AQUINAS101

This book is a gift for teachers of Catholic philosophy and theology. Now he can be studied by the "beginners" he cared so much for. And, thanks to Francis Selman, he can also be understood.

Mark Johnson, Ph.D.
Professor of Theology, Marquette University

Graced with clear, straightforward language and simple, fitting illustrations, this work enables one unfamiliar with Aquinas both to acquire a basic appreciation of St. Thomas's views and to relate those views to contemporary philosophical and theological discussions. Those seeking acquaintance with one of the greatest minds the Western world has produced will not be disappointed by Fr. Selman's excellent text.

Thomas Flint, Ph.D.
Professor of Philosophy, University of Notre Dame

AQUINAS101

A Basic Introduction
to the Thought of
Saint Thomas Aquinas

Francis Selman

Christian Classics ✦ *Notre Dame, Indiana*

Founded in 1865, Ave Maria Press is a ministry of the Indiana Province of Holy Cross.

www.christian-classics.com

ISBN-10 0-87061-243-3 ISBN-13 978-0-87061-243-5

Cover and text design by Brian C. Conley

Printed and bound in the United States of America.

Library of Congress Cataloging-in-Publication Data is available

To Sister Eustochium

Contents

Preface

This book arose from a set of talks that some students at Allen Hall, the diocesan seminary of Westminster, asked me to give. Rather than tell them what they could find in my first book, *Saint Thomas Aquinas: Teacher of Truth* (T & T Clark Publishers, Ltd.), I prepared for those talks by reading in quite new parts of St. Thomas, as though I had not read him before. The present book is thus quite different from my first. The chapters on angels, the emotions, the Old Law, and the resurrection have no counterpart in the first book. Although the chapters on creation, the soul, and the virtues retain the same titles as before, these too have been specifically written for this book. Many new details have been included throughout, especially from St. Thomas's commentaries on scripture. I could not avoid using old material altogether, but have tried to cast it in new perspectives. To help with the understanding of the philosophical terms that St. Thomas uses, I have provided a glossary at the end.

The book falls into three parts of nearly equal length: chapters one to five on God and creation, six to eight on human nature and action, and nine to twelve on the economy of salvation. If two themes emerge from what I have written, they are unity and love. These two come together in the final chapter on charity. "The teaching of faith is directed to this end," St. Thomas says, "that faith may work with love" (on 1 Corinthians c.2 lecture 1).

I wish to thank Laura Callaghan for typing the script, her sister Josie for some final work on the typescript, and Helen Carr at Veritas Publications for her kind and perceptive assistance as editor. The picture on the front cover appears through the very kind cooperation of Fr. Mark Crisp, Rector of Oscott College.

F. J. Selman May 2004

Abbreviations

CG Summa contra Gentiles
De Div. Nom. De Divinis Nominibus
De Pot. De Potentia
De Ver. De Veritate
Qq. de Virt. Quaestiones de Virtutibus in Communi
ST Summa Theologiae

Prologue

Although we come to St. Thomas because we are interested in his thought and writings, his life was not wholly uneventful. It was judged by his contemporaries to be remarkable enough to be recorded by three biographers within living memory of him. Dating the events of his life and his works continues to be almost a subject in itself today. Here, however, I shall sketch it as simply as possible, in order not to present a mass of facts and details at the very beginning. St. Thomas's life was marked by several long journeys, accomplished on foot, from southern to northern Europe and back, in between the main periods of his teaching and writing: from Naples to Paris, from Paris to Cologne and back, back to Italy, and once again to Paris and back to Naples in his last years. These journeys are not without their significance for St. Thomas's view of our life, which he often describes as one of *viatores* (travelers) on their way to their heavenly homeland. In the next life, he says, we shall be *comprehensores* (those who understand and behold what we have only dimly discerned by faith in this life).

St. Thomas was born in 1225, just one-quarter into the thirteenth century.[1] He came of noble stock, for his father, Landulf, was descended from the counts of Aquino, in the region north of Naples now known as the Campania. His mother's name was Theodora. Three events occurred at the beginning of the thirteenth century that were to influence the course of St. Thomas's life. First, the rise of the new universities in western Europe: Paris, Naples, Bologna, Oxford, and elsewhere. The last university had been closed by the Emperor Justinian at Athens in 529. This was a time, then, of great intellectual reawakening. Second, the whole corpus of the works of Aristotle became known in the West for the first time through Latin translations of the Arabic versions brought by Arab scholars into Spain via Northern Africa. Hitherto, Aristotle had almost only been known in the West for his works on logic through the commentaries of Boethius (ca. 480–524). Third, within the space of very few years, the beginning of this century gave birth to two quite new apostolic religious orders, the Franciscans and Dominicans, founded in 1209 and 1215, respectively. These two orders marked a new departure in the life of the Church because they were apostolic orders of friars who went out to preach and take the gospel into the cities, in contrast with the older monastic orders of monks whose lives were centered on their monasteries, often in the country. The friars also thought that they should be teaching at the heart of the centers of learning, in the secular universities.

This transition from the old to the new was also reflected in the life of St. Thomas, as he was to receive his first education at the hands of the Benedictine monks at Montecassino—where he was sent to school at the age of five or six, in 1231, before he attended university. When the presence of the emperor, Fredrick II, and his troops, made the area around Montecassino unsafe, St. Thomas was removed by his family in 1239 and sent for safety to Naples. At the university in Naples, St. Thomas had Peter of Ireland, who introduced him to the philosophy of Aristotle, as one of his lecturers. In Naples, he also met for the first time the newly founded order of St. Dominic, which he entered in 1244 against the wishes of his family, who had hoped that he would one day become the abbot of Montecassino and thus rule over widespread lands to the advantage of his family. When St. Thomas's prior decided to send him to Paris out of the reach of his family, his brothers intercepted him at the command of their mother near Orvieto, and he was imprisoned in the family castle at Roccasecca for over a year. But the young friar's resolve could not be broken, and he was allowed to continue on his way in the summer of 1245 to Paris, where he found St. Albert the Great already lecturing on Aristotle and using his thought in theology. Up to this time the chief philosophical influence on the thought of the Fathers and teachers of the Church had come from the side of Plato. In the West this was largely due to St. Augustine, who had been the dominant theologian in the Western Church for almost eight hundred years since his death in AD 430.

When St. Albert left Paris in 1248 and moved to Cologne to found a house of studies there, St. Thomas accompanied him. The relation between St. Albert and St. Thomas may be compared with the one between Haydn and Mozart. In both cases the pupil eclipsed his master in fame, but the master outlived his more brilliant student. In Cologne, St. Thomas heard St. Albert's lectures on *The Divine Names* by Pseudo-Dionysius. This author is so called because he was for a long time believed to be the Dionysius converted by St. Paul on the Areopagus in Athens,2 but is now recognized to be someone writing in Syria in the first decade of the sixth century, around 510. With St. Augustine and St. Gregory the Great, Pseudo-Dionysius is one of the three Christian writers most quoted by St. Thomas.

In 1252 after four years in Cologne, St. Thomas returned to Paris and began his own teaching career. From 1252 to 1256 he wrote his commentary on the *Sentences* of Peter Lombard (ca. 1100–1150). This was the standard textbook of theology at the time and was commented on by all St. Thomas's great contemporaries in Paris: St. Albert and the two Franciscans Alexander of Hales and St. Bonaventure. The *Sentences* displays the distinctive character of the scholastic method, which is to assemble the various opinions (*sententiae*) of the Fathers of the Church about any one question in theology, for instance whether God created the angels before or at the same time as the world, and to come to a reasoned conclusion about which opinion is to be preferred. St. Thomas was considered to be quite young for becoming a master of theology when he was just over thirty in 1256. For the text of his inaugural lecture he chose Psalm 103: 13, "You water the tops of the mountains from your dwelling place above." The mountains, he says, are the teachers and the water from above is the wisdom that God gives. The duty of the teacher is to pass on the wisdom he has received from above, but as no one is adequate to hand on divine wisdom by himself, he (or she) has to ask God for it in prayer. From 1256 to 1259, St. Thomas wrote his first major set of disputed questions, on truth (*De Veritate*). Before he left Paris in 1259, he had begun his first *Summa*, known as the *Contra Gentiles*, in which he sets out to demonstrate the reasonableness of the Christian faith. St. Thomas spent the next ten years in Italy, first at the papal court of Urban IV in Orvieto from 1261 to 1265, and then in Rome from 1265 to 1268 in order to set up a Dominican house of studies at the church of Santa Sabina. In Orvieto, he completed the *Summa contra Gentiles* and, at the request of the pope, compiled the *Catena Aurea*, a commentary on the four gospels consisting entirely of the texts taken from the Fathers of the Church. He also composed the hymns, responsories, and antiphons for the feast of Corpus Christi, which Urban IV instituted in 1264. During the three following years in Rome, he wrote the disputed questions on power (*De Potentia*), (1265–66), his commentaries on the *Divine Names* of Pseudo-Dionysius and on the *De Anima* of Aristotle (1267–68), his commentary on the epistles of St. Paul from chapter eleven of 1 Corinthians to Hebrews, and the First Part of the *Summa Theologiae*, which henceforth will be called the *Summa* as distinct from the *Contra Gentiles*. When we compare the *Summa* with the commentaries on the *Sentences*, we see how St. Thomas brought a simpler order and new clarity into theology, as it is altogether easier to find a reference in the *Summa*. The First Part of the *Summa* is on God and his creation.

In the summer of 1268, St. Thomas was recalled to Paris to combat the rising tide of students in the faculty of arts, who were following Averroes's interpretations of Aristotle with a disregard for their incompatibility with the Christian faith. Averroes (1126–98) held that when Aristotle calls the intellect separate, he means that there is a universal mind existing out-side of us and in which we all share. This view can still be found today, for example, in the scientist Erwin Schrödinger (d. 1961), who believed that we all have one consciousness. It clearly undermines the belief of Christians in the immortality of the individual soul because, if my mind is not really my own but an external one thinking in me, I am not responsible for my actions and so all meaning of reward or punishment in the next life for what I do in this life is removed.

St. Thomas also had to return to a fresh attack on the new religious orders by the secular masters in Paris, who were envi-ous of the friars when they took the chairs of theology. One crit-icism made by the secular clergy was that religious poverty is against mercy and charity because, by giving up all their posses-sions, the religious make themselves unable to help the poor. St. Thomas replied that as society needs members who are devoted to study and contemplation, because the highest end of human life is to know the truth, the religious dispossess themselves for a higher end than helping the poor by material means. The whole of society benefits from the spiritual good that a few of its members are able to gain by their way of life. St. Thomas points out that part of friendship is to assist one another in spiritual as well as worldly duties; indeed the former is more necessary for attaining our main end—beatitude in heaven.[3] Although the background of St. Thomas's life was not as calm and peaceful as the even and unimpassioned tenor of his works may suggest, it is possible to overemphasize the part played by controversy in his writing, since most of his third visit to Paris was taken up with the day-to-day teaching of the regular courses in scripture and theology.[4] The time when St. Thomas was most engaged in controversy was also the time of his greatest literary activity. Within the space of three years, 1269–72, he wrote the Second Part of the *Summa*, on moral theology, which takes up over one-half of the whole work; his commentaries on the gospels of St. Matthew (1269–70) and St. John (1270–72), the disputed ques-tions on evil (*De Malo*, 1270); and his massive commentaries on the *Metaphysics* and *Nicomachean Ethics* of Aristotle.

For commenting on the works of Aristotle, he had a fresh translation made directly from the original Greek by a Flemish Dominican, William Moerbeke. St. Thomas also set theology on a new footing in several ways. He made greater use than hitherto in the West of the acts of the first seven ecumenical councils, which for a long time remained in Greek and had recently become available in Latin. This brought a new dimension to his Christology—for example, in the questions on the union of the two natures in Christ and on his two wills, human and divine. St. Thomas's theology may be called truly ecumenical in that he frequently quotes the fathers of the Eastern Church—Athanasius, Basil, Gregory Nazianzen, and John Chrysostom—whom he primarily knew through the *De Fide Orthodoxa* by St. John Damascene (ca. 655–750), itself a kind of summa of Eastern theology. By the time he left Paris, after Easter 1272, in order to return to Naples, he had already written the first twenty-five questions of the Third Part of the *Summa*, on Christ and our salvation.

Once back in Naples, he worked on his commentary on Romans and continued the Third Part of the *Summa*, with the questions on the mysteries of Christ's life and the sacraments. But he was never to finish it, for on the feast of St. Nicholas in December 1273 he had a vision in which, as he expressed it, "All that I have written seems like straw compared with what I have seen." After that, he wrote no more. Early in the following year, he set out for the Council of Lyon, which Gregory X had summoned to discuss reunion with the Eastern Church. But not long into his journey he fell ill and, seeing that his end was near, had himself removed from his sister's house to the Cistercians at Fossanova, where he died on March 7, 1274. Thus, his life came full circle, and when he left Paris, in 1272, to return to Naples, it was really a homecoming, as he was to die near where he was born. After several great journeys in his life, and worn out by almost continuous teaching and writing, he who had been a traveler now entered the life of plain vision and comprehension of all that he had labored to put into words. He was canonized by Pope John XXII in 1323. His achievements as a writer and thinker, however, make us forget that he was also a saint. For it was from his daily life as a religious that his writings flowed: his humble obedience to his brethren; his devotion to Christ, always his first master; and his frequent recourse to prayer, from which he said he learned even more than he did from books.

1

How Can We Know God?

For St. Thomas, God is the beginning and end of everything; everything comes from him and returns to him. Theology for St. Thomas is first of all about God and only about other things in view of God, as they come from or go back to him. Thus, the first question for St. Thomas is about God. Contrary to those who think that belief in God is just a matter of faith, St. Thomas thought that we can know that God exists, beginning with our natural knowledge of things. In this way we can come to know that God exists as the cause of things. But he did not think that we can know *what* God is. As he says in the *Summa*, "because we do not know what he is, but what he is not, we cannot consider how God exists but rather how he does not exist."[1] When he says, "how he does not exist," he means not as a body, not finite, not changing, as visible things are, but infinite, immutable, and eternal. St. Thomas makes his own the sentiment of Pseudo-Dionysius: "we are joined to God as to the unknown."[2]

At present it is common to emphasize the negative aspect of our knowledge of God, which St. Thomas shares with the tradition of the Eastern fathers. But it is possible to exaggerate the negative theology of St. Thomas, as though we could not know anything about God. St. Thomas himself adds to the words of Pseudo-Dionysius quoted above, "we know him more fully, however, inasmuch as several and more excellent effects of his are shown to us and we attribute some things to him out of divine revelation, which natural reason does not reach, as that God is three and one." St. Thomas would hardly have said in the prologue to the second question of the *Summa* that the principal intention of sacred doctrine is to hand on a knowledge of God (*cognitionem dei tradere*) if he had thought that God remains completely unknown and inaccessible to us. He even thought that it would be contrary to divine goodness if God did not communicate to us some knowledge of himself.[3] What then did St. Thomas think we could know about God?

First it should be said that St. Thomas thought we can know about God in two ways: by reason and by grace. The light of reason itself is, St. Thomas liked to say, quoting Psalm 4:6, as though "the light of your face signed on us." Grace is an additional light, which enables us to know things that reason cannot reach by its own strength. This second way of knowing God is itself divided into two: faith in this life and the light of glory we need to strengthen our mind to see God in the next life. St. Thomas compares the knowledge that reason and faith give us in the following way: the doctrine of faith is a higher and more certain adherence than natural knowledge, although it is imperfect in explaining what is above the power of reason and our understanding. Faith adheres more certainly inasmuch as divine revelation is more certain than human knowledge.[4]

By the light of reason, St. Thomas says, we can know that God exists as the cause of the world, because effects resemble their cause and bear a likeness to their cause. Every piece of music by Mozart, for instance, bears the inimitable stamp of its composer. We have to start with created things in order to come to know about God by natural reason, St. Thomas says, because all our knowledge takes its beginning from the senses. Created things can lead us to know *that* God exists, but they cannot let us know *what* he is because they in no way match the cause of all things.[5] It is because created things are in some way like their cause that they allow us to know something about God, but because they fall far short of him that we cannot speak of created things in the same way. Thus, we can only speak of God by analogy. We draw an analogy between things when they are alike in some respect but differ in nature. We may talk about the moaning of the wind because it sounds like someone moaning, although the wind is quite different in nature from a human being. The philosopher John Locke tells us that some people fancy the idea of scarlet like the sound of a trumpet.[6] Although scarlet differs from a trumpet in nature as a color does from a sound, they may be likened one to the other by an analogy because the brilliant color of scarlet may have a similar effect on me as the piercing notes of a trumpet do.

Analogy

St. Thomas drew his doctrine of analogy from the *Divine Names* of Pseudo-Dionysius. St. Thomas's attention had first been drawn to this work by the lectures of St. Albert when they were in Cologne. Pseudo-Dionysius says that as God is hidden and beyond anything we can describe with words, we should think of God as much as he reveals about himself to us, and not say anything about his hidden divinity except what is expressed in the sacred sayings of scripture, which he says sheds a spiritual light like rays of light in our mind.[7] Pseudo-Dionysius observes that when we praise God as wise and almighty, good and strong in hymns, we apply names to him. We notice, by way of contrast, that St. Thomas thought we could name God not only from the sayings revealed in scripture but also from created things. Applying names to God raises two questions: If we can apply many names to God, is this not contrary to his simplicity? Should there not rather be one name for God? And second, as God is far above creatures, what knowledge of him can any of our words give us? St. Thomas makes clear that we do not know God as he is through the divine names, because he is ineffable and unfathomable; but they let us know God as the source and cause of the power, goodness, and strength in created things.[8]

In saying that we can speak about God by analogy, St. Thomas differed sharply from Moses Maimonides (1135–1204), who was a contemporary of Averroes in Cordoba until 1165, when persecution by the Moorish ruler in that city made him flee to Cairo, where he ended his days as father of the Jewish community and court physician to the caliph there. *The Guide of the Perplexed* was an attempt to reconcile Jewish faith with reason rather as St. Thomas later did for the Christian faith in the *Summa contra Gentiles*. Maimonides thought that God cannot be simple if he possesses attributes. Thus, he denied that we can say anything affirmative about God, in order to uphold his simplicity. All positive names for God, Maimonides declared, are equivocal: that is, we mean quite different things by them for God and for creatures, so that they do not really tell us anything about God. For instance, he thought that we use the word "exist" in altogether different ways about God and creatures. Maimonides did not think that there could be any analogy between creatures and God because he did not think that they have a relation to God. He also thought that to ascribe attributes to God implies that he has qualities.[9] In Maimonides's view, we can only speak about God negatively and the names of God are to be understood in a negative way, so that when we call God wise, we mean he is not ignorant. Only negations lead us to a knowledge of God, he says; only negative attributes are permitted, or if there are any positive ones, they apply to the actions of God.[10] St. Thomas, however, thought that we are not confined to negative names but can speak about God affirmatively because, as he points out elsewhere, every negation rests on an affirmation.[11] For example, you cannot say someone is ignorant unless you know what knowing is, or that something is insoluble unless you know what soluble means.

What then allowed St. Thomas to think that we can speak about God affirmatively by analogy when Maimonides denies this? We can see that there are two reasons. First, St. Thomas drew a crucial distinction between the way a word signifies and what it signifies.[12] How a word signifies, he says, is as we use it of creatures that we are familiar with and know more closely, but what it signifies belongs more to God since God is more truly good, or wise, or strong than any creature. Second, we can speak of God by analogy because creatures participate in God. We speak by analogy because God does not participate in anything, but creatures do. You cannot share in anything unless it exists before you. For instance, I share in human nature because I received human nature from beings who had it before me. But nothing exists before God, so that he can receive it from anyone or thing before him. This doctrine of participation comes from Plato: we find it well stated in the *Phaedo* 100c, where he opines that the things we see are beautiful because they share in beauty itself. St. Thomas's source for it was Pseudo-Dionysius. Maimonides, then, did not allow us to speak about God by analogy, because he lacked the doctrine of participation. St. Thomas, however, agreed with Maimonides that we cannot apply our names to God and creatures in just the same sense, or univocally, because God does not participate in anything but creatures do. When we say that creatures participate in God, we do not open the way to some kind of pantheism but mean that all the perfections we find in creatures, such as being good, wise, or powerful, derive from God as their source. On the other hand, if our names for God are merely equivocal, as Maimonides thought, St. Thomas did not see that there is any order or likeness of creatures to God.

We can speak of God by an analogy with creatures because they have a likeness to God, as all effects are in some way like their cause. Thus, we name God after creatures. We take our various names for him, such as "good" and "wise," from the diverse perfections that we find in creatures and attribute them to him as the primary source of those perfections.[13] Nothing that we know would be good or wise unless God were good and wise. He is the source of all perfections, which, as it were, come forth from God in what St. Thomas calls "the procession of creatures from God." We name creatures after God, St. Thomas observes, because we can only name things as we know them, and what we know first is created things.[14] What allows us to name him after them is that he is the source of every perfection in them:

"God is known through the divine names as their principle and cause."[15]

We speak about God by analogy, because the perfections of creatures exist in God in a far higher way as the source of them. The perfections in creatures pre-exist in God and creatures derive them from him by sharing, or participating, in them. We have to speak of God by analogy because these perfections exist in God and in creatures in a different way. God is not just wise, good, and powerful: he *is* Wisdom, Goodness, and Power itself. This is not true of any creature: they may be good or wise but none is Wisdom or Goodness itself. Solon was wise but is not Wisdom; wisdom is rather something that he shared in. When we call God "living," we speak by analogy because creatures are living but God is Life itself. This is because everything that receives something like existence, life, or goodness goes back to something that does not receive these perfections from another or, therefore, share in them. God does not share in life: he is Life; all life comes from him. Thus, speaking about God affirmatively by analogy is known as the "eminent way," because the perfections in creatures, after which we name God, exist in him in a higher manner.

When we name God from the diverse perfections in creatures, we do not, however, as Maimonides feared, take away the simplicity of God, since the perfections that are found in many creatures exist simply in God, for they are all one in him. This follows from the point I have just made above: as God is not just wise but is Wisdom, and not just living but is Life, not only is God identical with each of his attributes, but each attribute is identical with the others. If God is his wisdom and is his life, his wisdom is his life and his life is his goodness, and so on. Thus, the many names of God do not detract from his simplicity, because they all name one thing in reality. As St. Thomas says, the various names that we apply to God derive not from any diversity in God but from the diversity of perfections we find in creatures, which we then attribute to God as their cause.[16] The question then arises whether our different names for God really have a different meaning or whether we might as well use only one name for God, seeing that all our names mean the same thing in reality. St. Thomas's reply to this question is that although *what* our names signify is a single reality, they do so *in many respects*. They are not just synonyms, because they have diverse meanings in our mind, even though they refer to one thing in reality when applied to God.[17] God has created a great variety of creatures to manifest his perfections, because no one created thing could adequately represent the goodness, power, and wisdom of God. As St. Thomas says, there is only one adequate representation of the divine nature: it is the divine Word.

The Analogy of Being

We speak of God by analogy because created things are like God in some respect. They are like God, St. Thomas remarks, not God like them, just as we say that a portrait is like its subject, not a man like his portrait. The first way in which creatures are like God, he says, is that they exist. We use the verb "exist" for God by analogy, because created things exist, but God is also Existence itself. As St. Thomas says, God is Being (*Ens*) but they are only beings (*entia*) by participation.[18] This is because they receive, and so share in, existence. The English language allows us to bring out this difference between God and creatures quite clearly. God is simply Being, with a capital "B"; we would, or should, not call God a being with a little "b." Conversely, any created thing is a being but we do not call any created thing being by itself; it is *a* being. If we call God "a being" this would make him like other things, as though he were just one among other beings. Then we would be using "being" of God and other things univocally, not by analogy. This shows why it is inappropriate to talk, as some contemporary philosophers of religion do, about "a universe in which God exists," as though God were an item among other items in the universe and not greater than the whole universe. God cannot be an item in the universe, as it all comes from him.

St. Thomas saw what philosophy says about God as Being, or Existence, itself as confirmed by scripture in the passage where God reveals his name to Moses as "I am He who is" or, in the Latin version that St. Thomas used, quite simply "He who exists" (*Qui est*).[19] St. Thomas thought that this is the most appropriate name that can be given to God, because it does not in any way limit what he is but is the widest of all names.[20] We may now sum up St. Thomas's doctrine of analogy under the following five points. God is the source of all perfections in creatures. But we apply our names for these perfections to God by analogy, because they exist in him in another and higher way. First, they exist in God in an eminent way because he is not just living but Life itself. And second, following from this, the perfections that are multiple in creatures all exist simply in God, as he is identical with each of his attributes. As they are all one in him, who is their source, the names we attribute to God do not take away his simplicity.

The Negative Way

We can say some things of God affirmatively by analogy, as he is the cause of all creatures, and thus of every perfection in them. But we also speak of God negatively, because we do not know what God is. Indeed, the affirmative way leads to the negative way. First we have to speak of God by analogy, St. Thomas says, because what we name exists in God in a way that altogether surpasses the meaning of our words.[21] It is just because, when I call God good or wise I do not mean that he is good or wise just like created things, that I also speak of God negatively. For, in affirming that God is good, I may also deny this of him in that he is not good in any way that my words could express. The way in which we also deny whatever we affirm of God is neatly summed up for us by St. Thomas as follows:

> Just as the names we impose on things can be predicated of God because there is some likeness of created things to God, so too, as created things fall short in representing God, the names we impose can also be removed from God, and their opposites be predicated of him.[22]

The negative way, then, is also known as the way of removal (*via remotionis*). It is the reverse side of the affirmative way. The two ways are related, because we can impose names on God as creatures have a likeness to him, but we also remove them because creatures fail to represent God adequately. Thus, whatever we affirm about God also has to be taken away, because God is good but not good in any way we know or, therefore, can say. St. Thomas points out, however, that we do not speak of God negatively because of anything lacking in him but because God far *exceeds* everything that we can know.

To speak of God negatively is to say what he is not. St. Thomas gives three reasons why we cannot know what God is. First, the mind of no created being can see God by its own natural power, because God infinitely surpasses everything in nature. We shall only know what God is when we see the divine essence, but to do this, the mind first needs to be strengthened with the light of glory. Second, we shall never know God completely because we can only know something as it exists, but God's existence is infinite. Third, when we say what a thing is, we define it. To define it is to set limits to the way it exists, but there are no limits to God's existence. We narrow down something when we say that this living thing is an animal rather than a plant, and this animal a kind of cat, and this cat a lion rather than a leopard. As St. Thomas points out, the nearer we come to know what something is, the more differences from other things we add. But as we do not know what God is, we can only say how he is distinct from other things by negative differences. Thus, we cannot know what he is, but we have some knowledge of him by knowing what he is not.[23] For example, when we say that God is infinite, immutable, immense, we remove limits from his existence and say that he is not one of finite, measurable, or changing things.

The Divine Light

One reason why we do not know what God is, is that the divine light is hidden from us by its simplicity. We may use here an analogy with ordinary light, which also illustrates what we have said above about analogy. Just as we cannot see pure light by itself but only when it is reflected by other things in the various colors of the spectrum, so we do not know God as he is but speak of him from created things, which reflect their Maker. And just as pure light is refracted into the colors of the spectrum when passed through a prism, so God is reflected in the diverse perfections of creatures. As the colors of the spectrum can then be recombined into the original beam of pure light by being passed through a second prism, so the diverse perfections of creatures are one in their source. Thus, the many attributes we ascribe to God do not take away his simplicity. As Cardinal Newman aptly says: "the pure and indivisible Light is seen only by the blessed inhabitants in heaven; we have such faint reflections of It as its diffraction supplies."[24] As St. Thomas says, quoting St. Paul, if anyone could see God he could not express it. When relating his visions, St. Paul says that he heard words that could not be uttered (*arreta rhemata*, literally "unsayable sayings").[25] Our knowledge of God in the present life differs from what the saints share in the life to come. We cannot now see the essence of God but are instructed about him through the veil of words in scripture and by the likeness of his effects in created things.[26]

St. Thomas sums up what he says we can know about God in the present life with these words:

> We know God most of all as the unknown, because the mind is found to know God most perfectly when it is known that his essence is above everything it can apprehend in the state of this life; and so, although it remains unknown what he is, it is however known that he exists.[27]

Thus, we can know that God exists but not what he is. What we know of God is that he far surpasses anything we can know in this life. What St. Thomas says is not that we do not know God but that we cannot *comprehend* him.[28] Incomprehensible is not the same as unknowable. To comprehend something is to take in all of it, to get your mind right round it. St. Thomas says that we comprehend something when we know it perfectly. We cannot even know God like this in all eternity, for he is infinite and so always surpasses what we know, just as when you reach the horizon you find that another horizon lies beyond it. We shall never comprehend God, but even in this life, St. Thomas says, we can touch him (*attingere*) by faith.

St. Thomas would hardly have called faith "a light" unless he thought that it gives us some knowledge of God. "The light of faith," he says, "is as though a stamp of the First Truth on the mind."[29] Faith joins us to what is unknown and unsayable, not as though it is known, for then it would be plain vision, but "unspeakably and obscurely," for now we do not see clearly but "as though in a mirror." We are joined by faith to the ineffable and unknown—that is, to the divine truth, which surpasses all human speech and knowledge—otherwise we would have open vision but we see only as in a mirror.[30] By faith, however, we are joined to the unknown imperfectly, because we are joined to what is above the power of natural reason. "By the light of faith the mind is raised above itself in contemplation, in that it knows God to be above everything it knows from nature."[31] As St. Thomas notes, reason inquires but the understanding contemplates.[32]

If God were altogether unknowable, we would have to keep silence about him, for we would be quite unable to say anything. But this was not the mind of St. Thomas, who wrote a great deal about the question of God. St. Thomas, however, thinks that there is a place for silence when we consider God, "God is honored by silence, not because we do not say or ask anything about him but because we understand that we fail to comprehend him."[33]

The saints, he says, revere the unspeakable things of God with a chaste and silent mind.[34]

In this way St. Thomas resolves the apparent contradiction of saying that we do not know what God is, yet can speak of him affirmatively as well as negatively. When we name God and give him attributes, we mean that he is that and, at the same time, he is not that because he is so much more than anything we can say with our words. So we can name God, though he remains hidden and unknown. Thus, the God we can speak of by analogy remains the hidden God of Isaiah in St. Thomas: "Truly, you are a God who hides himself."[35] In the end we pass beyond reason, which only enquires, and come to contemplation that simply beholds him.

2

Creation

Creation is very much at the center of discussion at the moment: partly because some scientists have put forward new theories about the origin of the universe like the Big Bang theory, which seems to resemble creation; and partly because many have become aware of the need to preserve the natural world. Creation is a major theme in St. Thomas, too, because the only way we can come to know about God by reason is from the things he has created. A right attitude to creation was also important to St. Thomas in view of the Incarnation. For how could the Christian belief that God united a human body to himself appear reasonable unless the material creation is good in itself? Most discussion about creation today, however, offers no explanation of how the matter out of which the universe is made came to be there in the first place but presupposes the existence of matter. Thus, scientists and others are often talking not about creation in the proper sense but about the genesis of the world: that is, how it came to be as we find it from its initial conditions, not how matter came to exist. To create, in the proper sense, means to make out of nothing. One thing St. Thomas shows us when talking of the creation is the reasonableness of the Christian belief that the universe has been created by God out of nothing. St. Thomas explains that, when we say "out of nothing," we do not mean that nothing is what the world is made out of; rather we use the word "nothing" as not out of anything. To say the world is created means that it is not made out of anything but only by someone.

The starting point of St. Thomas's thought about creation is his doctrine that God is Existence itself, or subsistent existence (*esse subsistens*). We have already touched on this when, in the previous chapter, we said that the first analogy between created things and God is that of being: they are beings and he is Being itself. As St. Thomas says in what may be regarded as the key article of the whole *Summa*, if we are to single out one article alone, other things are beings by participation because they receive their existence from something existing before them, but God is not a being by participation, because he does not receive his existence from anyone.[1] Since God does not share in existence, he *is* his Existence. St. Thomas tells us that he got this thought from the Arab philosopher Avicenna (980–1037): everything that has existence must go back to something that simply is Existence. St. Thomas thought that there can only be one being who is Existence itself because, if there were another, they would have to differ in some way—just as if two things were whiteness itself, they would have to differ, and then at least one of them would not be whiteness itself.[2] From this it follows that there can only be one source of existence and God is the author of all existence.[3] For example, if by creation we meant that God gave order to matter which he did not produce, he would not be the author of all existence. St. Thomas also shows that the world requires a creator because matter cannot be the original principle of the world. Matter cannot be the origin because, he points out, it is not an active but *passive* principle in itself. Matter does not move unless it is first moved by something else. Thus, matter must itself be an effect of the primary active cause.

To Make Out of Nothing

Creation in St. Thomas's view means to make out of nothing; otherwise there is something that was not made by God but out of which he made things, and thus he is not the source of all existence.[4] Unless creation in the proper sense means to make out of nothing, there is no difference between our way of making and God's. We only make things by changing something that already exists, as someone cannot make a pullover out of nothing but requires some wool. But, as God is the source of all existence, there is nothing else already existent before he makes anything, nor does he make the world out of himself, as though it were an emanation of the divine being. Thus, as St. Thomas puts it, nothing is presupposed to the action of creating: "As God is the author of the whole of existence, nothing having existence is in any way presupposed to his action."[5]

From this two things follow. First, to create is to produce the whole substance of a thing, not just to give some matter a new form, which is the way we make things, but to make the matter as well.[6] To create is to bring something into existence as a whole, *simpliciter*.[7] It is to make the thing and what it is made of all in one. As St. Thomas puts it, God gives something existence and that which receives the existence together. Second, as creation in the active sense is not the change of anything, for nothing yet exists to be changed, it is instantaneous. St. Thomas vividly makes this point by saying that when something is created it is no sooner being formed than it is formed; it is formed and has been formed in one and the same moment.[8]

"The first of created things," St. Thomas says, "is existence." He took this phrase from the Book of Causes (*Liber de Causis*), proposition 4, which St. Thomas was the first to recognize as a selection from the fifth-century Platonist philosopher Proclus. He explains that existence is something created, not as though it were a "thing," but in the sense that color is the first of visible things because nothing is seen unless it is colored.[9]

The Neoplatonists

We only produce things as an individual. For example, two human beings produce a new human being but they do not produce a human nature; rather they too received human nature from their parents. When we take this back, we come to the question, where did the first human being or whale or first bird receive its nature from? It was as an answer to this question, St. Thomas thought, that Plato said it came from something he called the Man himself or the Whale or the Bird itself. These were Plato's Ideas, which he said all existed independently. St. Thomas, however, saw that the source of human nature, the whale nature, and so on must be quite other than any of these things.[10] Indeed, he saw that the source of the different species is not so many separate and independent principles, like Plato's Ideas, but is one Being, because there are not many principles of creation, so to speak, as in Plato, but only one. For Aquinas, everything in the universe comes immediately from the One, to use the term of the Platonists. This was quite unlike anything that the Neoplatonists thought. We shall now have to describe the Neoplatonist theory of creation and show how St. Thomas differs from them.

As the chief concern of the Neoplatonists was to preserve the complete transcendence of the First Being, whom they called the One, it cannot be the source of all being but must be beyond being or else it would be a being like other things. This made it necessary for them to suppose a series of intermediary agents between the First Being and the material universe, so that the universe is not the direct creation of the One or God. First, they said, the One by thinking of itself produced Mind. As Mind received its existence, there is some complexity in it, for it is passive as well as active. Then Mind produced Soul, which produced the material world in Avicenna's scheme, because the soul is the source of motion in bodies that can move themselves, that is, living ones. Some Neoplatonist schemes supposed a greater number of intermediary beings between the One and the material universe. As they came before anything material, they were immaterial beings and so intelligences. The Neoplatonists thought that matter could only issue from the lowest of these beings, but St. Thomas took the opposite view: far from matter being the product of the lowest of them, it comes from the highest of all. He thought that what is most general, because it underlies all things in the visible universe, must itself come from the highest and most universal cause. This is God.[11] As God produces matter, he also produces the forms. St. Thomas rejects the idea that angels had a hand in creation by putting forms into matter.[12]

The Neoplatonists did not overcome the difficulty of how you get to matter: they only deferred the problem. By ascribing it to the last of the series of intelligences descending from the First Being, they still had to suppose that it was produced from nothing and so created. But St. Thomas shows that the whole Neoplatonist scheme is impossible because no one but God can create. First of all, the scheme supposes that one immaterial being emanated from another, but St. Thomas points out that, as an immaterial being is not made out of anything, the only way it can come into existence is by being created.[13] But no being that is brought into being by another being has the power to create, because the gap between nothing and something is an infinite one, which only an infinite being has the power to cross. God's existence alone is not limited in any way, because he has not received his existence from another. Thus, St. Thomas argues that only God can create things. We may sum up his thought by saying, "nothing created can create," and, "creatures cannot be creators." This shows us what is wrong with Richard Swinburne's supposition that God could give some creature the power to create. This is impossible, because every creature is limited as it receives its existence from another. As St. Thomas points out, the Neoplatonist scheme still requires that the first corporeal body be created, because it has to come from nothing material before it, but none of the intelligences or emanations from the One has the power to create.

St. Thomas remarks that if the universe was not created directly from God but is the work of an intermediary being, then it would not be as God or the Primary Being intended it to be but the intention of an inferior being and could have evolved in a way he had not foreseen.[14] Nor would the universe be fully under God's control if it were not his intention, but this would be contrary to belief in God's Providence, which extends to everything in the universe. For St. Thomas the world is due to neither necessity nor chance but is intended by God.

Created by Free Will

A noticeable aspect of Aquinas's discussion of creation is the frequency with which he rebuts the idea that God created the world out of necessity and not out of free will. For St. Thomas the sole cause of creation is not any necessity in God to produce thought but the *goodness* of God. The goodness of creation shows that God created it freely, by will and not by necessity.[15] Aquinas had no need of the elaborate schemes of the Neoplatonists, because everything proceeds from God by thought and will. Doubtless, it was important for him to uphold the view that God creates by free will and not necessity, because this view frees us from the pessimistic view of the world of Neoplatonism and dualist religions as it enables us to see the goodness of creation. We see that creation is good when God creates by free will because God would only want to make something good. St. Thomas holds that God does not act by necessity of nature but by knowledge and understanding. As will always goes with intellect, for there is no being that has intellect but not will, which is against the idea of having a mind, so God creates by free will. God could not have produced the world with its great variety of things if he had created it by necessity, St. Thomas argues, because nature always acts in one way. For example, pear trees only produce pears, copper always dissolves in sulfuric acid, and wax always melts in the sun. As St. Thomas observes, it was because the Neoplatonists thought that the One could only produce one effect that they had to suppose a chain of intermediary beings in order to explain the great many kinds of things in the world. But for St. Thomas, the manifold effects of creation come directly from the Primary Being, not through a series of intermediary beings. He also argues that God creates by free will, not by necessity, because as we have dominion over our actions, how much more must God be master over everything that he does.[16]

By maintaining that God acts through intellect, Aquinas is able to overcome another difficulty of the ancient philosophers: how you get something from nothing, for they all held that nothing comes from nothing. Thus, many of them had to take the existence of matter for granted without offering an explanation of it. St. Thomas, however, frequently observes that everything acts in its own way. Now, as God acts by intellect, and intellect is immaterial, as we shall see in chapter six, God can make something from nothing. Since God acts by intellect and will, he can be the immediate cause of variety and diversity in creation, without any need for a series of intermediary causes, like the intelligences of the Neoplatonists. Diversity in the world comes from someone who does not act by necessity of nature but by will because, though nature acts in one way, the will is not limited to acting in one way but chooses between the various possible courses of action first seen by the intellect.

Aquinas further argues that God creates by free will, not by necessity of his nature, because nature acts for an end, otherwise it is the result of chance, as materialists have supposed ever since Democritus, because they do not think that it comes from a Mind that gives it order. Interestingly, materialist scientists today also suppose that there are many universes, in order to increase the chance of intelligent life appearing in one of them. St. Thomas, however, thought that there is order in the universe, because the regular motions of the heavenly bodies are plain for everyone to see. But order supposes an end, because one thing is only ordered to another if they are ordered to an end, as we notice in the structure of plants and animals, whose parts and organs are so ordered that they are able to reach their completed growth, maintain their life, and perpetuate their kind. Matter, however, does not act for an end that it sees, but in order to aim at an end you have to know the end. Thus, in St. Thomas's view, a world in which many things in nature pursue their end without knowing it must come from a Mind that has given things their proper ends. As an end presupposes knowledge, nature only acts for an end, St. Thomas says, because it is directed by an agent that wills its end. He thought that the true explanation of diversity in the world was neither necessity nor chance but the ordering of God's wisdom, which he saw manifested in the order of the world.[17] This explanation, he notes, is confirmed by scripture: "You have made all things in your wisdom" (Ps 103:24), and "You founded the earth by wisdom, with understanding you fixed the heavens" (Prv 3:19). Order, St. Thomas remarks, does not come about by chance. Diversity in the world, then, does not come from chance but from God, because one thing is fitted to another, so it must be intended. It is the intention of its Maker. Aquinas also notes that an agent directs things to an end by will. He points out that not only are things diverse but they also agree with one another; one order, however, can only come from one cause that coordinates everything, not from chance.[18]

St. Thomas's firm adherence to the view that God creates by free will also sets him against two philosophers of the seventeenth century, Spinoza and Leibniz. Spinoza held that as everything created expresses the attributes of God, the world resulted from the necessity of God's nature. If God created by free will, Spinoza maintained, God's attributes could be otherwise than they are. Spinoza also objected that the will of God is identical with his essence but his essence cannot be otherwise than it is or there would be more than one God.[19] Spinoza's explanation of freedom was that God alone is free because only he exists by the necessity of his *own* nature. It also follows that if God creates by necessity, he is bound to create the best of all possible worlds, as Leibniz maintained. This too would impose a constraint on God's activity. St. Thomas, however, held that God does not create out of any necessity, because he is not obliged to make a world. From this, it follows that he does not have to make the best possible world but only one in which everything is given what it needs to work well. As St. Thomas points out, God does not owe anything to creation but everything he gives it is unowed.[20] God does not need to create a world because he is self-sufficient for his own happiness. In St. Thomas's view, God is his own happiness (*beatitudo*); the creation of the world did not add anything to God's happiness, but, as a result of creation, he shares it with other beings. God cannot depend on anything else to make him happy, or else he would not be the First Cause.

St. Thomas is also able to show that it is not against the simplicity of God that diversity comes directly from him, as the Neoplatonists thought. As God has an idea of everything he makes, God has many ideas, but this seems to be against his simplicity and oneness. St. Thomas acknowledges that many ideas in God would be against his simplicity if his ideas were caused by other things, but this is not so, for God's ideas are rather the cause of things in the first place.[21] Thus, St. Thomas thought that we do not have to suppose that God created by means of a series of intermediary beings in order to safeguard his simplicity, as the Neoplatonists supposed.

Immanence and Transcendence

As St. Thomas does not need to invent a series of intermediary beings in order to preserve the complete otherness of the First Being, he is also able to show that God is immanent in the universe without compromising his transcendence. For many throughout the ages immanence and transcendence have been incompatible: God is either immanent and so part of things, with the result of pantheism; or God is so far above things that he is altogether remote from them. Spinoza took the first of these two ways; the Neoplatonists the second. For St. Thomas, however, God is removed from things in the way he exists because he also *is* his existence, whereas everything else shares in existence; but God is not remote in that he is cut off from other things. Indeed, St. Thomas thought that God is at the heart of all things, because he is the cause of their existence, and nothing is more intimate to a thing than its existence. Its existence is the inmost aspect of it, St. Thomas says.[22] In his view, God is in all things, because he holds them in existence every moment by his power. As the whole series of causes and effects in the world depends on God for its existence in the first place, so it would cease to exist if for one moment he withdrew his continued support from it.

God's Knowledge of the World

If God were cut off from the world, as the Neoplatonists held, he would not know particular things and events in the world but only have knowledge of the world in a general way— for instance, he would have knowledge of the laws of nature but not of actions by particular things, or have the ideas of species of animals but not of individual animals. This, however, is against God's Providence, as it is revealed to us in scripture. God's knowledge of the world is not just general, because his Providence is particular. For example, God is said to know and scrutinize our thoughts. Even pagan philosophers of antiquity could see that if God does not know particulars, he knows less than we do. But God cannot be ignorant of anything that we know or else he would not be most wise. Here a problem arises, for how can God know individuals when the proper objects of the intellect, according to Aquinas, are universal concepts? St. Thomas's way of dealing with this difficulty is to draw a comparison with the builder's knowledge of the house he builds. A builder does not know a house by its art, St. Thomas says, but only when he sees a house with his senses. The builder does not produce the matter out of which he constructs a house by his art but only the form of a house in the matter. But God can know individuals, although he only knows things by intellect, because he produces the matter as well as the form of things. The likeness in God's mind of the thing he knows is not received from the thing but is rather productive (factiva) of the thing, for things come from God's knowledge in the first place.[23] In this way God knows individual things as well as universals. Thus, anyone who does not think that God produces matter immediately but by intermediaries, as the Neoplatonists held, will have a difficulty about how God knows particulars as well as universals. From this we see that Providence, which includes knowledge of particulars, goes with creation, God's direct making of things. God has providence of single things, like a sparrow, not just of universals as human rulers do, St. Thomas says.[24]

To the mind of some critics, one weakness of St. Thomas's thought about creation seems to be that he does not sufficiently relate creation to the individual persons of the Trinity.[25] St. Thomas would have replied that all three Persons act insepara-bly in their operations outside. He would also have thought it too strict the demand that everything be explicitly related to the Trinity, since this requires us only to discuss things in a way that presupposes faith, whereas the strength of St. Thomas is that he also approaches topics of theology in a way that is accessible to those who do not have Christian faith and that can be recog-nized by reason. Even so, as Gilles Emery observes, Aquinas links creation with the Trinity, for he says that "the divine Persons have causality in respect of the creation of things by rea-son of their processions." As God creates by the concept of his intellect and by his will, he has made creatures by his Word, who is the Son, and by his love, who is the Holy Spirit.[26]

Is the World Eternal?

Anyone who thinks that the world is due to necessity must also think that it is eternal. Although Aristotle thought that there must be a First Mover who is the source of motion in the universe, he thought that the world has always existed because he did not see why the First Mover should move the world, not having moved it up to that point.[27] Aristotle also presupposed the matter of the world; his First Mover is not also the Creator of the world but only explains why there is motion in it. St. Thomas, however, against Aristotle, thought that you could demonstrate by reason neither that the world is eternal nor that it has a beginning, as some of St. Thomas's contemporaries in Paris thought. We cannot show that it is not eternal, St. Thomas argues, because there is nothing in things to show that there has not been an unending succession of them. Nor can we show that it has a beginning, because if it is not necessary, it depends on God's will for coming into being, but we only know about God's will through revelation. Thus, St. Thomas thought that we only know that the world has a beginning by faith; it is not something you can prove by reason.[28]

St. Thomas's doctrine of creation derives from his view of God as the source of all existence, since God alone is his existence. It is against the very idea of God's making of things that he requires anything else existent, because he would no longer be the source of all existence. Thus, when God creates the world, he makes it out of nothing. The diversity we find in the world comes neither from necessity, for by nature one thing acts in one way, nor from chance, because the world would not have order. Nor does it come from intermediary beings, as the Neoplatonists supposed, because they cannot create. Thus, God created the world by free will. As the universe comes directly from God and is his intention, we see that it is also good. So we turn next to St. Thomas's idea of the good.

3

Good and Evil

We saw in the previous chapter that God is the source of all existence and that everything that comes from him is good because he created it by free will, not by necessity. In this chapter, we shall consider what St. Thomas means by calling things good. We shall also consider the opposite of good, that is, evil. Evil plays a notable part in the thought of St. Thomas, perhaps because the religious order to which he belonged was initially founded by St. Dominic, to preach against the Albigenses in Languedoc in southwestern France. These Albigenses, named after their stronghold in the city of Albi, held a variant form of the heresy of the Manichees, named after their founder, Mani, who lived in Persia in the middle of the third century. The Manichees were dualists, because they held that the material world does not come from God the creator but from a second source of existence, a malevolent being. They taught a dualism of matter and spirit, ascribing these to two separate sources: spirit is good and comes from God; matter is inherently evil because it comes from a principle of darkness. St. Dominic saw that it was vital for Christianity to uphold the goodness of creation because any view that regards matter as evil strikes at the central mystery of Christianity, the Incarnation, by which God joined to himself a human body, a part of his material creation. The Manichees therefore denied that Christ had a real human nature and held a form of Docetism, saying that his body was only an imaginary one and thus that he did not really suffer on the cross but only *seemed* to.

Before we see how St. Thomas combated the heresy of the Manichees about the source of evil, we should first look at what he says about the good, for it not possible to understand evil, which is negative in itself, without considering it in relation to something positive. As evil is nothing in itself, we cannot say what it is without first turning to its opposite, the good. We can only assess evil in comparison with the good, just as every denial presupposes an affirmative. For example, you cannot say what poor or bad leather is unless you know what good leather is. For St. Thomas nothing is inherently evil; everything is good inasmuch as it exists, because God is the one source of all existence.

Good and Being

The question whether good or existence is primary has recently been reopened. In Plato, the good seems to be the highest of the Ideas and to have the position of God.[1] The Platonists put the good first because for them the One, or God, was beyond all being as it was important that the first cause could not be anything of what it causes. This is why they say that existence is "the first of created things," a saying of Proclus that St. Thomas used, as we saw in the previous chapter. Although St. Thomas was at one time generally held to be wholly Aristotelian in his philosophy, it has now become increasingly common to recognize the Platonist elements in this thought. It seems to me, however, to be going altogether too far to regard Aquinas to be as much a Platonist as he was an Aristotelian. When Aquinas mentions Plato it is almost always to criticize him, except for the doctrine of participation, which is Platonist, but St. Thomas's source for it was Pseudo-Dionysius.

The Platonists put the good before being, because it is the first cause of acting. As Aquinas himself often remarks, the first cause of action in time is the final cause, why we act: we first have a purpose or intention before we set about achieving it. For example, in order to make an engine I first need to think of its purpose, in other words, of its end. St. Thomas was faced with the question of whether good or being is primary when he read Pseudo-Dionysius, who puts the Good first because it is identical with God but says that being, or existence, is the first of God's effects ("the first of created things"). St. Thomas agrees with him that the good comes first as the end of action, what things act for: they act for the desire of something good. But he comes down squarely on the side of saying that existence comes before the good, because a thing is good inasmuch as it exists. Existence is prior to the good because existence is the first good that is sought by everything; the first thing everything seeks is to preserve its existence. For St. Thomas, there is a way in which the Platonist position is right, and another way in which existence is prior to the good. In reality, he says, existence and the good are interchangeable terms.[2] When it is a matter of knowledge, existence comes first because you cannot know anything unless it first exists. But from the point of view of causing things, the good comes first as the good is the end for which things act.

Although the good and existence are interchangeable in reality, good and being are not mere synonyms. In their idea or concept, St. Thomas says, good and being differ: they are the same thing in reality but differ in meaning, because we look at reality from various aspects. St. Thomas remarks that Pseudo-Dionysius puts the good first, because he says all our names for God refer to him as he is the cause of the perfection in creatures from which we take our names, as we saw in chapter one, and good is the first as the cause of acting. But St. Thomas maintains that existence is prior to good, because a thing can only be known as it exists.[3] As he often remarks, being is the first thing that comes into the mind; whatever we say about a flower or an insect, for example, we first of all think that it exists. In weighing St. Thomas's view against that of Pseudo-Dionysius, Fran

O'Rourke points out, in favor of Aquinas's view, that the first name of God is not the Good but "he who exists" (Ex 3:14).[4] For the Platonists, God is the Good but not Being, because they thought that he is beyond all being. Although the Platonists put the good first, because the final cause is the first in the stages of acting, St. Thomas observes that a cause does not cause anything unless it first exists. Thus, the good precedes as the end is prior in the order of causes (why we act in the first place), but being is the condition of anything being a cause at all. Being is also an even more universal idea than good, in St. Thomas's view, because the first idea that comes into the mind about anything is that it exists.

The Notes of Goodness

St. Thomas's view of the material order is well summed up by St. Paul's saying to Timothy: "everything created by God is good."[5] When writing to Timothy, St. Paul seems to have had in mind people who held a dualist heresy like the Manichees later, for he tells us that they despised marriage. We find five notes of the good: (1) all *being* is good; (2) things *seek* the good; (3) they are good as they are *perfect*; (4) the good is their *end*; (5) they are good because they have a *likeness* to God.

(1) Everything is good inasmuch as it exists, because it comes from the one source of all existence, God, who is good.[6] Everything that exists is good, St. Thomas says, because it shares in existence, and the source of existence is good.[7] Thus, "good" and "being" are interchangeable terms in the same way as "true" and "being" are also interchangeable terms. The existent is true as it is known, and good as it is desired. To be good, however, is not quite the same as to be: being is good as it is *desirable*.[8] We see from nature that the existence of a thing is good, because everything by nature loves its existence and strives to preserve it. Its being is its first good. Whatever threatens or harms its life is apprehended as bad for it, for example, poisonous substances. Being is good, St. Thomas notes, because everything that has existence naturally loves its existence and strives to preserve it as though it were something good.[9] When fish are

taken out of the water, for example, they struggle to remain alive by breathing. As living creatures love their existence and strive to preserve it, this leads us to the second note of goodness in St. Thomas: it is what things seek.

(2) Aristotle defines the good as "that which all things seek."[10] The powers with which living things are equipped to seek what they need to preserve their lives are called "appetites." Things are good as they are *appetibilis*. We notice that when people have lost their appetite for living, they also lose their appetite for what preserves their life, for food. Something is good inasmuch as it exists, but living things cannot just remain in existence without also exercising their powers. Thus, there is something more for them than just existing: they strive not only to preserve their existence but also to exist fully by realizing their various powers. In other words, they aim to reach complete existence, which is to perfect their existence. This brings us to the third note of goodness: perfection.

(3) A thing is perfect when there is nothing lacking from its proper nature and existence. But things have different ways of being perfect. There is more to being perfect for human beings than there is for dogs or dolphins, because with our intellect we are able to think of so many more ways of acting. Our perfection obviously lies in the exercise of our highest powers, the intellect and will; thus, in St. Thomas's view, our perfection is to know the True and love the Good. As things are not only good in their existence but perfect when they achieve their full existence, we come to the fourth note of goodness in St. Thomas: the good is the end of things.

(4) When living beings, including humans, seek and strive to obtain what they apprehend as good for them, they act for an end. We see that things act for an end in nature: for example, the end of a caterpillar is to turn into a butterfly because its nature is to become a butterfly. Things are good when they attain their end, as a good pear tree bears fruit and a pear tree that bears no fruit is defective. Only what is good is the end we seek in acting; evil is never an end in itself. Nothing seeks what it apprehends as bad for it, but avoids it. We can do evil, however, in seeking

something that is good in itself when it is not directed to our proper end. Pleasure, for example, is good in itself, but not when we make it the end of our life because the senses are not the highest part of our nature; it needs to be directed to its proper end in our life.

Everything has been given an end in nature, and to reach its end is its good. But nothing created is its own end because it is not its own goodness but shares in goodness, just as it shares in existence, which it has received from another. God alone is his own goodness, and everything else is good by participating in goodness.[11] As God is his own goodness, there is no end beyond God, but God is the end of all other things. Nothing else is its own end, or an end in itself, because there is always some greater good beyond it.

This view of God as the end of all things has two consequences for St. Thomas. First, everything seeks God in seeking its own good, because all goodness derives from God.[12] Many things in nature do this without knowing it, unconsciously as we might say; but some do it knowingly, and these are also beings with will. Thus, second, beings that have will are good when their wills are directed to God. Actions done with a will that is not consonant with the will of God cannot lead us to our proper or last end but only away from it. God, however, does not act for an end, because he is goodness itself; there is no end beyond God. Thus, he acts solely out of his goodness in order to communicate his goodness to creatures. As St. Thomas frequently says, quoting Pseudo-Dionysius, "goodness diffuses itself"; it is of the nature of goodness to pour out and spread itself. Dualist views of the world and philosophies that regard the world as an illusion tend to have a pessimistic attitude to the world, but, contrary to these, St. Thomas sees the goodness of God poured out in all creation.

(5) As everything seeks God in seeking its own good, it seeks God not only as its last end but also as its First Cause, because everything has been given its end by its Maker. This brings us to the fifth note of goodness in St. Thomas, that things are good because they are like God. Everything bears some likeness to

God because an effect is like its cause. No cause can produce an effect that lies altogether outside its power or is, therefore, quite unlike itself. But some things are more like God in their nature than others: we more than other animals, angels more than us, because they are pure spirit. As effects resemble their cause, the goodness of creatures is a reflection, and so a likeness, of God, in whose goodness they all share, each in its own degree. By seeking their own perfections, they seek God inasmuch as the perfections of all things are a certain likeness of the divine existence (*esse*).[13] Creatures are like God as he is the source of their goodness, and in seeking their good, they seek God. Thus, God is the beginning and end of all things for St. Thomas. He is their beginning as everything comes from God, the source of all existence; he is their end, for everything returns to him as it seeks God in seeking its good.

Evil

Seeing that everything comes from God, who is good, one may now ask how there comes to be so much evil in the world as we find it? One answer, as we have already seen, is that material creation does not come from God but is the work of some malevolent being. St. Thomas, however, scotches this view, because God is the only source of existence but evil does not come from God. It follows, then, that evil in itself cannot be anything existent. As it is not anything existent, evil cannot be a primary principle because nothing comes from nothing. If things are bad it is not because they exist, but it must be in some other way.

We may divide the question of evil into three: What is evil? Where does it come from? Where do we find it?

Evil is the opposite of good. As all being is good, because it comes from God, evil cannot be anything existent; it is rather a lack of being. We see that things are bad or evil, because they harm or take away from the full existence of something. For example, acid is bad for the skin because it destroys it. As St. Thomas points out, evil only corrupts things; it does not generate them.[14] This means that evil cannot be a cause of things existing. Thus, there cannot be a principle of evil as there is a principle of good, namely God, because what is wholly evil would not exist at all, as evil is a lack of existence. Nothing recedes wholly from the good; otherwise it would cease to exist altogether. Nothing can be wholly evil, then, and the Manichean idea of an evil being who is the source of the material world is impossible. As St. Thomas affirms, there is only one source of existence: God is the origin of all existence (*origo totius esse*).[15] Everything comes from one principle, not from two, as the Manichees held.

The source of evil is not a principle of evil or a rival being to God. Nor is it God. Could nature be the source of evil? St. Thomas rejects this possibility, because nothing is essentially evil, for evil is what is against something's nature. Everything evil is good in its essence. It is a contradiction to say that something is bad by nature, for evil by definition is opposed to its proper being. If something were evil by nature, it would be good for it to be evil, but this would be a contradiction because nothing can be against its nature. Nothing is bad by nature, St. Thomas says, but evil arises from a defect of what ought to be present by nature. For example, the inability to see is counted as an evil in creatures that are meant to see; blindness is not an evil in a stone, St. Thomas remarks.[16] Thus, we cannot properly talk about a cause of evil; rather it is due to the defect of a cause. As St. Thomas notes, virtue is the perfection of a power, and evil weakens the use of a power. To take another example of St. Thomas's, the evil of lameness springs from a defect of a power in the leg. As evil is the defect of something, it is not anything existent in itself. Evil does not come from nature, St. Thomas says, but arises when things do not keep the order of their nature.[17] As evil cannot exist by itself, for nothing can be wholly evil, evil is only found in things that are good by nature.

St. Thomas thought that defects can occur in two ways. First, nothing created is perfect, since it does not have perfect existence but shares in existence. He does not mean not perfect in its own way but not perfect in the way that God alone is perfect being. The second way is by free choice in creatures with will.

No one chooses evil, as it is evil, for everything only seeks the good, but we choose things because of what is good about them. For example, revenge is sweet, but it is only partly good because it would be bad for society if people took it into their own hands to administer justice instead of turning to an impartial judge. As St. Thomas remarks, we usually do evil for the sake of some apparent good.[18] To choose evil is, for St. Thomas, due rather to failure of the power of will, since it then becomes less free. Evil in angels and human beings comes from the aversion of the will from God, which is by nature subject to him.

Since evil takes away from a thing's existence, and all existence is good, evil is a *privation* of the good. Things are good by sharing more in goodness, but they are not evil by sharing more in evil, for evil is nothing in itself. They are evil by sharing less in the good that is proper to their nature. Thus, evil does not come from a single source in the same way as all goodness derives from God; rather it is due, as St. Thomas remarks, to many defects.[19] There is only one right answer to a problem in arithmetic but many ways in which the answer can be wrong. Thus, the good has a unity, and evil lacks unity; rather evil will destroy the unity of a thing as it breaks it down or corrupts it. For St. Thomas, something has being as long as it is one being.[20] For example, a clock only exists as long as all its parts have unity. Likewise an animal or human being only exists as long as its members have their unity. St. Thomas observes that a good example of disunity arising from evil is the human emotions when they are not ordered by reason.[21] When our emotions are not in accord with reason, they conflict with one another, and we experience a lack of unity in ourselves. As unity strengthens, for we act better when all our powers act in concert, so evil weakens our power to act. As we have already noted, virtue perfects a power, and evil weakens its operation.

Since St. Thomas finds that nothing is evil in nature, and nature acts in one way, as we noted in the previous chapter (one chemical always reacts in the same way with the same other one), he comes to the conclusion that evil springs from beings that can act in various ways. These are beings with will, who can think of or choose alternative ends; they do not have to act in the same way. Thus, the source of evil is wills that are opposed to God. Actions are bad when they are not ordered to their proper end; in other words, when they are disordered. St. Thomas sees a certain similarity between moral goodness and health: as health consists in a good state of the body and disease arises from some disorder in it, so the will is bad when it is not rightly ordered. In an article on pain as a form of sorrow, St. Thomas remarks that the greater evil is not pain but to be separated from God.[22] What separates us from God is not physical suffering. Guilt is a greater evil than pain, for it makes someone bad simply speaking, but pain not so. St. Thomas thought that not to shun evil or to think that evil is not evil was worse than pain.[23] It is a greater evil to be deprived of right reason. Guilt alienates us from God more than pain, because God is not the author of guilt but is of punishment as part of justice. To be deprived of grace and glory is a punishment as well as pain is. This is what makes the question of evil so difficult, says St. Thomas.[24] He remarks that sin diminishes our nature just as grace perfects it. Creatures are related to grace, as the eye is to the sun for the light it depends on to see anything.[25]

Providence

Evil, however, raises a problem for belief in divine Providence, which I said at the beginning of this chapter covers all things. For it would seem that evil cannot be part of God's plan and, therefore, evil does not come within Providence. St. Thomas saw in the steady course of the heavenly bodies a sign that the universe is ruled by providence and a supreme intelligence. Nonetheless, he admitted that human affairs do not seem to be ruled by providence, since good and evil are allotted to the just and the unjust alike without any apparent respect for what each deserves. He thought the sufferings of the innocent to be the greatest obstacle to belief that human affairs are ruled by divine Providence. The difficulty comes, St. Thomas points out, in thinking that reward and punishment are only meted out in this life, which he says is where the friends of Job erred.[26] That we are not rewarded for good or repaid for evil in this life shows, in St. Thomas's estimation, that the last end of man does not lie in this life. St. Thomas gives three principle reasons why evil is not contrary to Providence but falls within it.

First, evil is not caused by God, since it is not anything existent; rather it comes from a defect of something existent. Second, God is able to make use of evil for his ends in Providence, although he does not will the evil in the first place. He uses the evil of pain and punishment, St. Thomas says, to correct sinners, to give an example of what befalls those who do not correct their ways, and to restore the good of justice.[27] Evil too becomes an occasion of virtue in some. Job proves his patience when God permits him to be afflicted. Providence uses evil for good. A physical evil resulted in the spiritual good of a conversion in St. Ignatius of Loyola. Likewise, imprisonment leads to a conversion in St. Francis of Assisi. Unless Joseph had been sold by his brothers to some Ishmaelites, he would not have been brought into Egypt and so have come into a position where he could help his brothers when they came down into Egypt in a time of famine at home.

Third, God permits evil because Providence preserves nature. As God has created some beings, angels and humans, with free will, he only respects the nature he has given them in allowing them to act freely. They would not be truly free unless it were possible for them to turn away from God as well as toward him by their free choice. As St. Thomas says, it is by Providence that the rational creature is variable.[28] For reasons that we will see in chapter five, angels are not variable after their first choice of will. Thus, evil is not against Providence in the divine plan. God does not intend the evil that is freely done, nor does he hinder it, because he lets us act according to our nature, which is voluntary. Thus, evil falls within Providence, which upholds the nature of things.

Beauty

To return now from evil to the good, everything is good in its existence, as God is the source of all existence. If anything is evil, it is not because it exists but because of a defect in its existence. Good is the end of all things, because they only seek something as it is good. Nothing created, however, is its own end or goodness, because it shares in goodness. God alone is Goodness itself, from whom all created things derive their goodness. Everything that comes from God is compared by Pseudo-Dionysius with the rays of the sun. God diffuses goodness in everything, he says, as the sun diffuses its light. Commenting on Pseudo-Dionysius, St. Thomas says that as the light of the sun cannot be seen directly by us, because it is too bright, but is seen on the edge of the clouds or the tops of the mountains when they are lit up by the sun's rays, so we cannot behold Goodness itself on account of its surpassing brilliance, but we see rays of it in created things.[29] Perhaps St. Thomas had seen similar sights of mountaintops lit up at sunrise, and of clouds at sunset, as he walked along the roads from Italy to France and back. For St. Thomas, as for Pseudo-Dionysius, created things are an express likeness of God's goodness, which come from him like rays from the sun. "The beauty of the creature is nothing other than a likeness of the divine beauty, participated in by created things." "They have all been made to imitate the divine beauty in some way."[30]

St. Thomas defines beauty quite simply as, "that which pleases the eye of the beholder."[31] His three marks of beauty are consonance, clarity, and proportion. Consonance goes with order, clarity with form, and proportion with quantity. The proportions of a Georgian house, for example, are pleasing to the eye. Both consonance and clarity come from God, who orders all things and is the fount of light. Every form participates in the divine brightness, St. Thomas says, because it is form that makes things intelligible, and so light, to us. A painting without any recognizable form in it is unintelligible to most people. The particular aspect that beauty adds to goodness is that it is apprehended by the intellect. We discern with the mind the agreement and proportion of the parts of a thing: for example, the radius of an arch to the height of the columns that support it or the composition of a picture. The beauty of the mind itself lies in its concord, or agreement, with truth. Thus, St. Thomas's view of beauty is quite contrary to the tendency of contemporary art to portray the ugly rather than what has light and consonance. For St. Thomas, art has essentially to do with beauty, one of whose marks is clarity. As he observes, "No one cares to fashion or represent anything except for its beauty."[32]

God has poured out his goodness on all creatures. The first thing he communicates to them is his existence. This is their natural goodness. There is, however, a higher kind of goodness, which he only communicates to beings with intellect and will that are capable of receiving it. This is grace. Drawing on 2 St. Peter 1:4, "He has granted us great and precious promises, so that we may be made sharers [*consortes*] of the divine nature." St. Thomas often describes grace as a participation in the divine nature. He says that we have a share in the divine nature "by a certain likeness."[33] By giving us a share in the divine nature, God "deifies" us or makes us like him.[34] In the next chapter, we shall see how we are in the likeness and image of God and how our likeness to God is also a likeness to the Trinity.

4

Word and Image

St. Thomas says that there are some things we can know about God by reason and other things that we would not know about him unless they had been revealed to us. The first of these is that God is one and three, the Trinity. As we can speak about God by an analogy with created things, so St. Thomas builds on the analogy of the mind used by St. Augustine (AD 354–430) to set forth the mystery of the Trinity. St. Augustine remarks: "the mind is mindful of itself, understands itself and loves itself; if we discern this, we discern a trinity, not indeed God but an image of God."[1] St. Thomas, however, uses St. Augustine's analogy in a new way, for instead of considering the three powers of memory, understanding, and will, to show how the Father, Son, and Holy Spirit are equally God yet God is one, St. Thomas focuses on just two of these powers—understanding and will— and shows how two persons proceed in God. At one stroke, St. Thomas presents a wholly dynamic account of the Trinity, based on the mind's *activities* of thinking and willing, and gives his account a scriptural orientation by beginning with the processions of the Son and the Holy Spirit from the Father, for which he clearly has in mind two key verses in the Gospel of St. John:

"I have come forth from the Father" (8:42) and "the Spirit of Truth, who proceeds from the Father" (15:26). In writing about the Trinity, St. Thomas is always conscious of the same spirit with which the Fathers of the Church approached the mystery. The Fathers were compelled to discuss the Trinity, he says, "however modestly and reverently, without presuming to comprehend." Although the Trinity is far above anything we can understand of it, an inquiry into it is not useless, for it lifts up the mind to grasp something of the truth and excludes error.[2]

St. Thomas, following St. Augustine, can use the analogy of the mind for the Trinity because, as Augustine noted, we are made in the image of God in the mind.[3] The particular use that St. Thomas makes of the analogy is to show how something can come forth yet remain within God, unlike creation in which something comes forth that is external. First, we should look at what St. Thomas says about how something is an image. An image is a special kind of likeness. There are two kinds of likeness. Every effect is like its cause, as we noted in the previous chapter, for a cause can only produce something that lies within its power. Things without mind he only calls *vestigia* (traces) of God. Only beings with intellect and will are said to be in the image of God. As there are two kinds of likeness (vestige and image), so there are two kinds of image. A thing is an image when it has the same form as something else. Thus, signs outside inns called "The Swan" show a painted image of a swan. But this image is not an image of the painter that produces it. Another kind of image is when someone produces something with the same form as him- or herself. This kind of image is produced by generation. In this way, a child is an image of the father and mother. This kind of image is of the same *nature* as what produces it. The only image of God in this way, St. Thomas says, is the Son of God. We are only images of God, he says, as an image impressed on a coin is like the prince or ruler who issues it, but we do not have the same nature as God. St. Thomas points out that the image of God does not lie in the essence of the soul, which has other powers, like sensation, that go with our corporeal nature, but in a power of the soul, namely the mind.[4] We are not in the image of God in our nature but in our *activity* of knowing and loving. This is a higher kind of likeness than a work of art is of the artist, for a work of art does not imitate the artist in his or her activity, as we do our Maker in the activity of the intellect and will.

The Word of God

For St. Thomas's doctrine of the Trinity, we may first go to question 9 of the *De Potentia*. There he notes that we attribute to God everything that is most noble in creatures. Thus, there is understanding in God.[5] Understanding is by a likeness of a thing one is thinking of. It should be said that the verb *intelligere* in St. Thomas does not just mean "to understand" but very often "to think of." When we think, the mind conceives something of what it is thinking of, which we call a concept. A concept is a likeness of what the mind thinks of. When the mind forms a concept of what it is thinking of, the concept comes forth in the mind. As St. Thomas says, thinking ends in a conception.[6] The concept comes forth, yet can remain in the mind. It can also be expressed outwardly by a word. But as our words express the conceptions of our mind, these conceptions may be called "words" first of all. For example, the word "primrose" expresses the conception I have in my mind when thinking of a primrose. In thinking of something the mind forms something: "The word is properly that which the thinker forms in thinking."[7] The mind's conception may first of all be called a word, because "there is no word without a conception."[8] St. Augustine, however, calls the conception in the mind an inner word, "a word of the heart" (*verbum cordis*), to use his phrase. Why he calls the conception of the mind a word of the heart can be understood from the way scripture sometimes means the mind when it speaks of the heart. This is clear when it speaks of the "thoughts of the heart" (Gn 5:6). King David is told to do all that is in his heart (2 Sm 7:3). Plans are in the mind rather than in the heart. Jesus asks the Pharisees why they question in their hearts (Mk 2:9), and St. Paul prays that "the eyes of your heart may be enlightened to know" (Eph 1:18). In these two instances, the heart stands for the mind, since it is the mind that questions and knows. Thus, the conception of the mind is a word of the heart, an interior word. But St. Thomas specifies that the outer word does not so much express the conception of the mind as the thing or reality itself that we are thinking of by means of the mind's conception; otherwise words would just stand for our ideas and not for things themselves.[9] The likeness in the mind of the thing it thinks of is an interior word that may be expressed by the sound of an outer word.

As the concept that the mind forms in thinking of something may be called a word, so the concept that God has in thinking of himself is called the Word. There are, however, three important differences between the inner word in our mind and God's Word. First, God does not form his Word; it always is. Second, our word is not identical with ourselves. And thirdly, God has only one Word. God does not form his Word as we form ours because his mind is not first potential. It is not potential, because God's activity of thinking is identical with his existence; thinking does not add anything to his existence, for he is always thinking. As God does not form his Word, it is eternal: it has always existed. If God's Word were not eternal, his mind would be potential to begin with, like ours. From this follows the second point: God's Word is identical with his mind, and so of the same nature as God, because his thinking does not add anything to his being but is his existing. As St. Thomas observes, the Word does not differ from the Father in nature but only in relation. There is a relation because the Word proceeds from another. St. Thomas sees all these points summed up in the opening verses of St. John's Gospel: "In the beginning was the Word [the Word is eternal] and the Word was with God [in relation], and the Word was God [of the same nature]."

The third point is that God has only one Word, because he thinks of himself, and thus everything else in his mind too with a single conception. There is only one act of thinking in God, because his thinking is not other than his existing, and it is perfect. The Word comes forth in God's thinking of himself, as a conception, or inner word, comes forth in the mind when we think of something. God's Word, however, expresses the whole Trinity, since the Father speaks all three divine persons in his one Word.[10] As St. Thomas says, the Son is the Word who perfectly expresses the Father.[11] One might ask why the Word is a distinct Person in God when all three Persons, Father, Son, and Holy Spirit, think of and love one another. St. Thomas answers that there is a relation of the Word to the Father, because the Word proceeds. St. Thomas explains that the Word is God understanding not as God producing or begetting the Word, for it is the Father who begets the Word, but as the Word proceeding from the Father.[12] As the divine Persons are only distinguished by their origin, in coming from another, but are alike in every other respect, so the Word proceeding is said of God personally, St. Thomas says: that is, the Word proceeding is a divine Person, whereas God's wisdom, for instance, is not a person because it is common to all three persons. Each one is wisdom, but only one is the Word proceeding. As what comes forth from us naturally is said to be generated by us, so what comes forth in God's understanding of himself is called the Son of God. God's Word is begotten because what comes forth of the same nature is said to be generated, but it is not made or produced. God's Word is not formed because God was never without his Word, just as he is always unchanging by thinking of himself. The Son of God is begotten but not made, for God's understanding is identical with his existing, so that the Word is God. The Word is the Son because what proceeds as a likeness and with the same nature is said to be begotten. As this Word is not accidental to God, for his thinking is not additional to his existence or to his mind, it is something subsistent in God. Thus, the Word is a distinct Person in God, because whatever subsists in intelligent nature, St. Thomas says, is what we mean by a person. St. Thomas says that what is signified by the word "person," namely subsisting in intelligent nature, *properly* belongs to God.[13] Although some authors today deny that we can apply "person" to God because we have a different concept of person, it is worth remembering that we owe the concept of person to the controversy about the Trinity in the fourth century in the first place.

The divine Word expresses not only the whole Trinity but everything else, too, because in thinking of himself God thinks of everything in his mind. God thinks of everything in one thought, because he sees everything in a single glance. God does not pass from one truth to another as we do in discursive reasoning, for this would be against his simplicity; but he simply intuits everything at once. As God thinks of himself and everything else in one act, he expresses everything by one Word, St. Thomas says, which is expressive of everything in God.[14] God's thought is one because, unlike our thoughts, God's thought is not caused by other things but is the cause of other things existing: "He spoke and they came to be" (Ps 32:9). God's thought is the cause of everything else because nothing would exist unless God first had a thought of it, just as a craftsman first has a thought of what he or she intends to make. Thus, God makes everything by his Word: "not one thing came into existence that did not have its existence through him [the Word]" (Jn 1:3). God makes everything by his Word because the Word is the conception that comes forth in his mind as he thinks of everything else in thinking of himself. St. Thomas explains that the Word is not an instrument with which God makes everything but God makes everything according to the concept of it in his mind.[15] We may note here the difference between the Christian doctrine and Plato's of the origin of the world: in Plato the world is made according to many separately existing ideas, but the Christian doctrine is that the world is made by the one Word (*Logos*) of God. But the Word is a likeness of the divine nature and of other things in different ways. The Word is the image of God, but it is the exemplar of everything that God makes according to the concept of it in his mind. The Word is called the image of God because he is the perfect likeness of the divine nature. The Word is, St. Thomas says, a likeness of creatures not as their image but exemplar.[16] The exemplar in the divine mind may also be called the archetype. The idea that an artist or inventor has of what he or she is going to make is also the exemplar of the thing.

The Love of God

As the Word comes forth in God thinking of himself, St. Thomas says that the Word proceeds in God by way of the intellect. Since intellect and will go together, there is a corresponding procession in God of the will. This is of love. The procession of love in God is the Holy Spirit. What proceeds in God by way of the will as love is called the Spirit, St. Thomas says, because love is an impelling force just as breath or a wind moves things. Interestingly Hebrew and Greek each have one word for breath and spirit, *ruah* in Hebrew, *pneuma* in Greek. The procession of the Holy Spirit, however, differs from that of the Son, so that they are distinct in their origin because the Son proceeds from the Father alone but the Spirit proceeds from the Father and the Son, as he is the love of them both. For the Spirit to be distinct from the Son, St. Thomas says, one must proceed from the other as well as from the Father. The Son does not proceed from the Spirit but the Spirit from the Son, because love comes from understanding rather than the other way round. Nothing is loved unless it is first known, St. Thomas repeats, following St. Augustine. We naturally love to know and love our knowledge. In the same way, the Word that comes forth in God as he thinks of himself is "a word breathing forth love" (*verbum spirans amorem*).[17] Augustine says that the Word is knowledge with love.[18] Obviously, God loves himself as he also thinks of himself, for he is the supreme good and so supremely lovable.

But what proceeds in God loving himself is not called an image of God, as the Word is, because there is not a likeness in the will of its object, as there is a likeness in the mind, or intellect, of what it thinks of. This is because the end of thinking is that something is in the mind, but the end of willing is rather that the will is *inclined* to its object. So it is called the Spirit, St. Thomas says, as breath, like air, moves and stirs. To breathe into is to inspire; so what is breathed is spirit.

> But since what is loved exists in the will as inclining and, in a certain way, impelling the lover from within to the thing loved, but the impulse

of a living thing from within pertains to spirit, so
it belongs to God proceeding by way of love to
be called the Spirit.[19]

St. Thomas takes care to point out that the Spirit is not the
love by *which* the Father and the Son love one another, as
though the Spirit were the principle of their love, but he is the
Love proceeding from them.[20] The Person who proceeds as Love
proceeds from the other two loving one another; he is Love
springing from them. He does not proceed from the mutual love
of the Father and the Son but is their love proceeding from
them.

What proceeds in God by way of the will, St. Thomas says, is
Love, because every act of will is rooted in love. We saw this in
the previous chapter, as things only seek the good. What is true
of natural things is but a reflection of what first goes on in God.
And just as God's Word is of the same nature as himself, since
his understanding is his existing, so what proceeds in God by
way of the will is also God, for his willing is likewise identical
with his existing (it is not anything additional to it).[21] But the
Word is distinct from the Spirit because they differ in the way
they proceed, as the Word comes from one, the Father, the Spirit
comes from the Son as well as the Father, just as love comes
from understanding. The love that comes forth from the Father
and the Son in their love of one another is breathed forth by
them both. St. Thomas also argues that as God has will and
every act of will is rooted in love, so there is Love in God. This
Love constitutes a person in God because it is subsistent love
and what subsists in intelligent nature is, by definition, a person. Love is subsistent in God because his act of willing does not
add anything to, but is identical with, himself.

A fine summary of St. Thomas's teaching about the Trinity is
contained in just one article of *De Potentia*, q.9.9. He starts with
the argument of Richard St. Victor (d. 1173) that we can know
by reason that God is a Trinity, because the perfection of divine
happiness requires love. As love requires another, God is not a

single person, but there is more than one in God. Charity, however, is not perfect if there are only two because love is not exclusive either, so it admits a third. But St. Thomas thought that only
faith assigns three Persons to God. He then proceeds to show
how God is one although he is also three, and why there are
only three persons in God, not more. St. Thomas first establishes, in keeping with the insistence of the Greeks on the divine
monarchia, that God cannot be one unless there is only one
source of it. Thus there can only be one who is unbegotten in
God, who is the Father. If there are others in God, they proceed
from the Father by some activity. This can only be by some
immanent activity; if it were by transitive activity, it would result
in something outside of God and so not be of the same nature.
The activity that remains within the agent is that of the mind or
intellect. Thus, others proceed in God by the activity of intellect
and will as his Word and Love. God's Word and Love are subsistent, because his thinking and his willing are identical with his
existing, or with his being, as we might say. What subsists in
intellectual nature is a person, so there are three Persons in God.
There is only one Word and one subsistent Love in God because
he thinks of and wills everything in a single act. If God did not
think of and will everything in a single act, that would take away
his simplicity. As God's act of thinking and willing remain within him, because they are the source of everything else, the circle
of thinking is concluded in God, and there are not more than
three Persons. St. Thomas adds that it is appropriate that the
Holy Spirit proceeds from the Father and the Son because two
are needed for love.[22] Thus, the double procession of Spirit,
known as *Filioque*, in no way undermines the *monarchia*, the single source of the divine nature, that the Greeks were so concerned to safeguard.

The analogy of the mind shows that the Persons who proceed in God remain within; they do not emanate from God but
proceed in him. St. Thomas notes that there is an increasing
degree of interiority from the lowest to the highest of living
beings. The lowest form of life is the vegetative life of plants. The
only thing that comes forth in the activity of plants is external

when they put forth new plants by generation. In the next stage of life, the sensitive life of animals, the reverse occurs when something external is made internal by sensation and imagination. But in the highest form of life, which is self-reflection, both the origin and the end of the activity are internal, for the conception that comes from the mind thinking of itself remains within the mind. There are, however, different levels of self-reflection, for the conception in our mind is not identical with our mind as God's is with himself, for our mind is potential to begin with, so that a thought is additional to it, but God's thinking and understanding are identical with his existing.[23] As St. Thomas says, when God knows and loves himself, God is in himself as the known and the loved because his knowing and his loving are identical with him. Thus, the Word and the Love that comes forth in God as he knows and loves himself are subsistent, and so divine Persons.

In thinking of himself, God begets a perfect likeness of himself, who is the Word. To beget, or generate, is to communicate one's own nature. When the Father begets the Son, he communicates the whole of his indivisible nature to the Son. Thus, the Father is in the Son, as the whole of his nature is in the Son. And the Son is in the Father as the one fount, or source, of the divine nature.[24] Although St. Thomas finds it easier to show that this is so for the Father and the Son, the same must also hold for the Spirit, as the Spirit comes forth from them as their Love and they breathe their Love in one another. The unity of the divine nature is secured, because there is one source of it, the Father, who does not proceed from anyone. The divine nature remains undivided in the procession of the Son and the Holy Spirit, because God's understanding and loving are identical with his existence. This communication of divine nature with the Son and the Holy Spirit in God's thinking of and loving himself is the source and pattern of God's communications of his life and love to use by grace, which St. Thomas describes as "a participation in the divine nature" (2 Pt 1:4). But we only have it by a participated likeness.

God's Dwelling in Us

St. Thomas makes the indwelling of the divine Persons in one another the model of their dwelling in us. First, the two persons who proceed in God by way of the understanding and will are sent into the world. These are the visible missions of the Son and the Holy Spirit. The Son was sent by the Father into the world by his Incarnation; he appeared visibly as man. The Holy Spirit was sent into the world when he appeared as a dove at the baptism of Christ, and as tongues of fire at Pentecost. As St. Thomas points out, the missions of the Son and the Holy Spirit do not mean that they were not previously in the world, since God is present everywhere, but that they were not in the world visibly. Only the Son and the Holy Spirit are sent into the world; the Father is never said to be sent in scripture because he does not proceed from anyone. The visible missions of the Son and the Holy Spirit were temporal, that is, only lasted for a time. But they continue to be sent into the hearts and minds of those who know and love God. These are the invisible missions of the Son and Holy Spirit. Again, St. Thomas remarks, the invisible missions do not mean that God was not in us but that he is present in a new way by dwelling in us by grace. God is in all things but only said to "dwell" in creatures capable of receiving his grace. St. Thomas points out that the whole Trinity dwells in us, although only the Son and Holy Spirit are said to be sent because you cannot have any one of the divine Persons without the other two, as each is in the other. Likewise, when Christ says that the Father and he will come to make their dwelling in anyone who loves him, the Holy Spirit is included, because the Father and the Son are nowhere without their love.[25] God dwells in us, St. Thomas says, as what is known exists in the mind and what is loved exists in the lover.[26]

The Son is sent to us invisibly when we know God, just as the Son proceeds in God understanding himself. Similarly, the Holy Spirit is sent in us when we love God, just as the Holy Spirit proceeds as the Love of the Father and Son. We cannot have the Son without the Holy Spirit because we cannot know God, St. Thomas says, without loving him. Although they are distinct Persons, they are also inseparable. The Son is sent to us not through any ordinary understanding but through an understanding that results in love. Thus, the pattern of our knowing and loving God is the Word breathing forth love (*verbum spirans amorem*).[27] Although the Son and the Holy Spirit are sent together in us, their invisible missions are distinguished by their effects of grace. These effects of grace in us correspond with the different ways that the Son and Holy Spirit proceed: by way of the intellect and the will. As the Son proceeds by way of the understanding, he enlightens the mind when we know God. And as the Holy Spirit proceeds by way of the will as the Love of God, he enkindles our affections with the love of God. As no English phrase can reproduce the contrast of St. Thomas's words, I give the Latin: the Son produces within us an *illuminatio intellectus*, and the Holy Spirit an *inflammatio affectus*.[28] Thus, the divine missions affect the whole person, mind and heart together. By the effects of grace of each mission we are made more like the divine Person who is sent in us. We are made like the Son as we know God, and like the Holy Spirit as we love him. St. Paul's phrase about being conformed with Christ is extended by St. Thomas to the Holy Spirit.[29] We are conformed with the Holy Spirit, he says, by charity. The primary effect of the Holy Spirit in moving us toward God is that he makes us lovers of God.[30] When we love God we are assimilated to the divine Person who proceeds as Love himself.

In his commentary on the Gospel of St. John, St. Thomas tells us more about the distinction of the missions of the Son and the Holy Spirit, and at the same time shows us how they work inseparably together. As the Son is wisdom begotten and the Truth, so the effect of his mission is to make us participators in the divine wisdom and knowers of the truth. The Son hands on to us the teaching of the Father, since he is the Word, but the Holy Spirit makes us receptive to his teaching. The Spirit gives interior understanding. The Son leads us to the Father, but St. Thomas says the effect of the mission of the Spirit is to lead us to the Son.[31]

St. Thomas's account of the Trinity shows us that, although the intellect seems to have the primary place in his thought, in the end he thinks that it is only completed by love. Charity perfects the image of the Trinity in us.[32] The image of God is made complete in us when we are made like the Holy Spirit; it is charity that makes us more perfectly in the likeness of the Holy Spirit.[33]

5

Angels

No book on the "Angelic Doctor" would be complete without a chapter on angels. St. Thomas is called the "Angelic Doctor" either for the purity of his life or for the way he wrote about angels, which is notable for the restraint and soberness of speculation about them. We find two approaches to the angels in St. Thomas. In the *Summa*, they are introduced as the highest part of creation, most like God in their nature. In his treatise *On Separate Substances*, they are placed rather within providence. Providence is itself God's rule of the universe, guiding it to an end. It has two aspects: one is the plan (*ratio*) of it in the mind of God; the other is the execution of this plan. Thus, providence is a disposition in God carried out by his angels. These two aspects may be compared with our distinction between the consultative and executive powers in government and the administration of justice. In carrying out the plan of his providence, God does not act directly in everything, but he makes use of *secondary* causes to execute his will. He has made these secondary causes to act freely: they are intelligent beings with free choice—angels and human beings, "The angels are the universal executors of divine providence."[1]

Immaterial Substances

Although we only know about angels from revelation, St. Thomas thinks that reason itself would expect some immaterial beings to exist in the universe, for we observe a scale of being in the world from inanimate matter up to intelligent beings. Unless we are to suppose that there is nothing higher than ourselves but only God, it is reasonable to think that there are other beings, who are intelligent like us but immaterial in nature like God, whose action is purely immaterial, by thought and will. St. Thomas argues that since God produces his effects by intellect and will, the perfection of the universe requires that he makes some beings who are just intelligences, for they will be most like the Cause of all things in their nature and way of acting. St. Thomas starts from the principle that all creation is good; what makes a thing good is its likeness to God. In St. Thomas's view, the goodness of creation requires the existence of beings who are like God in having incorporeal nature.

Although it is hard for us today to think that any such beings could exist, St. Thomas thought it reasonable to think that there are immaterial beings like angels, because we know that our minds are immaterial. His argument for this is quite direct. Material things exist here and now, in this time and space, as we would say; they are particular. But we can also think of them *generally*, which is not how they exist in themselves here and now. It is therefore to think of them *immaterially*. The mind could not think of things in an immaterial way unless it was itself immaterial. For example, all horses are particular and individual, but I can also have the idea of a horse and think of what a horse is without thinking of any particular horse: this is to think of horses generally. He concludes that as we can tell that our own thinking is immaterial, it is possible for there to be some beings who have been created immaterial in their nature.[2] He points out that to say that only those things exist that we can imagine is to say that we are confined to the imagination; in other words, nothing exists except what we can have images of. But we know that there is a higher way of knowing things than by the senses, which only know things as they exist here and now, for we can also think of them generally. St. Thomas reminds us that to think there is nothing immaterial was the error of the Sadducees.[3] When St. Thomas taught that the angels are purely immaterial, he was opposing many of his contemporaries, who thought that angels either have "aerial" bodies or at least consist of what they called "spiritual matter." St. Thomas argues against the existence of aerial bodies that, if any parts of air are animate, all air would be animate. But no body can be airy because air has neither shape nor limits.[4] St. Thomas traced the error about angels consisting of spiritual matter back to its root in a book known as the *Fons vitae* (Fount of Life) by a Jewish philosopher, known by his Arabic name of Ibn Gabirol (ca. 1021–1058). Ibn Gabirol thought that unless angels consisted of matter, they could not be distinguished one from another and would be infinite because form by itself is infinite and only made finite when received by matter. St. Thomas, however, shows that Ibn Gabirol's fear was unnecessary because, although spiritual substances are not finite from below like material ones, they are finite from above, because they receive their existence.[5] Although an angel's form is not limited by matter, it is limited to a particular nature. St. Thomas is of the mind of scripture that angels are pure spirits: "Are they not all ministering spirits sent forth to serve?" (Heb 1:14)

The Creation of Angels

As angels do not consist of any matter, they are immaterial substances. An immaterial substance is an individual being with activities of its own that is not united to a body. An immaterial substance therefore is just a form. It is possible for something to be just a form, because it is form that gives existence to matter anyway, according to the philosophy of Aristotle. Matter is never found just on its own but only exists with some form or other. The belief that some things are pure forms or immaterial substances is not confined to Christian thinkers but is already found in ancient philosophy. Plato thought that his Forms, or Ideas, were immaterial objects existing on their own. Aristotle thought that the motion of the heavenly bodies required some immaterial substance to explain it. As matter does not move unless it is moved by something else, what moves the heavenly bodies unless it is some substances that are not material? Both Plato and Aristotle thought that their immaterial substances were eternal: Plato, because Ideas are unchanging, so they have no motion; Aristotle, because he thought that motion has no beginning. They had to think that they were eternal because neither had any idea of creation from nothing. Against Plato and Aristotle, Aquinas thought that there were no eternal substances. Since angels are immaterial beings, and so not made out of anything, they can only come into existence by being created. It follows from this that one immaterial being cannot emanate or derive from another, because an immaterial thing does not have parts, and so cannot begin as part of something else. Thus, all angels come directly from God, who is the immediate cause of every single angel. As we noted in chapter two, this doctrine is quite unlike the Neoplatonist scheme of the world from a series of immaterial beings, the intelligences, emanating one from another.

The Fathers of the Church were divided in their opinion about whether the angels were created before the world or simultaneously with it. St. Gregory Nazianzen held the former opinion; St. Jerome took the latter line. St. Thomas sided with St. Jerome. In favor of this view, he points out that there is just one universe of visible and invisible creatures. The angels are part of the same universe as we are: they are the invisible creation.[6] As they are part of the same creation, it is reasonable to suppose that they were created together with the corporal creation.

What Angels Are

For many people today the idea of an immaterial substance must appear to be a contradiction; if something is a substance, it is material. This was the view of Thomas Hobbes (1588–1679).[7] Before we question how something could just be a form without matter, we need to alter our usual view of substance. Most people think that when you take away form from substance, what you are left with is matter.[8] To Aristotle, however, it appeared the other way around: form is substance without matter. Form is the principle of existence of matter, as we have noted just above, because form makes matter exist as some kind of thing: for example, matter as copper, and copper as kettle. A form can exist on its own if it has some kind of activity. This will be an immaterial activity. In the next chapter, on the soul, we shall show that thinking and understanding are not the powers of anything material. We have already seen that when we think of things generally, this is not as they exist in matter, which is individual, but immaterially. An immaterial substance can exist, then, by intelligent activity. St. Thomas notes that angels are called intelligences because they have no other power, but their intellect is not their essence (only God *is* his mind or intellect).[9]

For St. Thomas, angels are intellectual substances not united to bodies. He also thought that a human soul is an intellectual substance, the lowest of them, which is meant by nature to be united with the human body. Although St. Augustine was prepared to think that the bad angels have bodies,[10] Aquinas held that all angels are immaterial. Evil, he said, does not lie in matter but in the will. St. Thomas supports the view established by Augustine in Book III of the *De Trinitate* that when angels appeared with bodies in the Old Testament, as to Abraham "who entertained angels unawares,"[11] they assumed bodies. Aquinas differs from Augustine, however, for Augustine says that the appearances of angels in the Old Testament are epiphanies of now this, now that person of the Trinity; but Aquinas says that all these apparitions are ordered to the Incarnation, for by assuming bodies the angels prefigured the assumption of human nature by the divine Word.[12]

As angels differ from human beings in their nature, for they have an incorporeal nature, so they differ in the way that they get their knowledge and know themselves. As angels do not have the bodily senses, they do not get their knowledge directly from material things but from above by being illuminated by higher minds or by God. If angels acquired ideas from material things, St. Thomas says, they would need the powers of the senses. As they lack these, they know things by ideas that are "connatural" to them.[13] An angel also thinks of itself through itself, because it is immaterial. We do not know ourselves directly through intuition but by reflecting on our activities, including the activities of our mind, but an angel knows itself directly through its essence, as St. Thomas puts it, because it does whatever it does with the whole of itself. Being immaterial means it does not have parts.[14]

The Hierarchy of Angels

In Christian tradition the angels have been divided into a hierarchy of nine orders, three sets of three. The first set comprises Seraphim, Cherubim, and Thrones; the middle set, Dominations, Virtues, and Powers; the third set, Principalities, Archangels, and Angels. The angels here are the guardian angels, who come last as they are nearest to us, having the immediate care of human beings. St. Thomas follows the order given by Pseudo-Dionysius in the *Celestial Hierarchy*, against the order of St. Gregory the Great in *Forty Homilies on the Gospel XXXIV*. The main difference between the two is that St. Gregory reverses the positions of Virtues and Principalities, so that he puts Principalities in the middle of the second set, and Virtues at the top of the third set. Thus, Pseudo-Dionysius has Dominations, Virtues, Powers, and Principalities; Gregory, Dominations, Principalities, Powers, and Virtues. Pseudo-Dionysius has the authority of Ephesians 1:12. Gregory, of Colossians 1:16 (Dominions, Principalities, Powers).

These orders of angels are distinguished by their activities and offices. Although not all their roles are clearly defined, certain distinctions are commonly ascribed to some of the orders. The three sets of orders can be divided by saying that the first reflects the attributes of God (who is love, knowledge, and justice); the second, his government; and the third, the execution of his providence.[15] St. Thomas sees the first set of three as concerned with the highest cause of all, the middle set with universal causes, and the third set with special effects of providence. St. Gregory says that the middle set is for the whole order of creation, the lowest set for human beings. In the first set the Seraphim represent the love of God, as their name comes from the Hebrew for "burning" or "ardent." St. Thomas says that the Seraphim are the highest order because they come next to the Holy Spirit, who is the Love of God. The Thrones stand for the throne of God's judgments; God executes his judgments though the Thrones. Following the order of Pseudo-Dionysius, the Virtues have power over corporeal nature, and the Principalities power over the human race and rulers of the kingdoms of this world. The Virtues command lower orders to execute their command over corporeal nature. This second set has the disposition of the order of the universe; the third set carries out the execution of this work. Principalities preside over the governing of nations and kingdoms. Archangels are the messengers of God, and angels are entrusted with watching over individual human beings.[16] St. Thomas explains that it is part of providence that angels are assigned to the care of individual human beings but not to other animals, because with animals only the species is perpetuated but every individual of the human species survives perpetually because of the rational soul, which is immaterial and so incorruptible, as we shall see in the next chapter.[17] Broadly speaking, then, we can say that angels of the first three orders are closest to God's secrets; those of the second set are rulers over the more universal powers; and the orders of the third set, over human beings. Interestingly, Plato divided his ideal state into three classes (rulers, guardians, and craftsman), and we commonly divide society into three classes: upper, middle, and lower (the working class).

Since an angel is just a form, and a different form is a different kind of thing, no two angels of the same order belong to the same species, but every angel is its own species. Things are either distinguished by being different lumps of matter or by having a different form. Thus, there is just one individual in every species of angel, for one angel differs from another by its form. But this does not stop angels from being individuals. Every angel is a unique species, as though there were just one dress made from every pattern. When we call them all "angels," we use angel not as the name of a species like "lion" or "leopard," but as name of a genus like "animal" or "flower," which includes countless species.

St. Thomas, in agreement with scripture (Dn 7:10), thought that there is a vast number of angels, "ten thousand upon ten thousand," as there is of species in the animal or plant world, because angels are better in their nature. We can define the nature of angels, but we cannot define their specific differences, because we cannot see them in this world. But the difference between one species of angel and another must be one of intellect, for they have a purely intellectual nature. St. Thomas thought that they differ in species, or kind, by the perspicacity of their intellect. They are diverse by diversity of intellect.[18] In contrast with our present emphasis on the quantity of information available, the distinction of angels lies rather in their power to see things more or less *simply*. The stronger the intellect, the more things it can think of with fewer principles. God thinks of everything with one concept, and the nearer an angel is to God, the simpler it is.[19] As God thinks of everything in one, so the higher the angel, the more simply it understands, with fewer and more universal ideas. In a similar way a professor is able to relate the knowledge of his subject with fewer key ideas than a student. Likewise, the more simple and elegant a law of nature is, the *more* phenomena it accounts for. The higher the angel, the greater its power of seeing all the conclusions contained in an axiom. We have to argue from step to step to discover conclusions by discursive reasoning, but an angel, properly speaking, does not reason: it simply sees things by intuition. They do this by the light of their intellect.

How Angels Speak

To speak is to manifest one's thoughts to another; "speech is a manifestation of the inner word," St. Thomas says.[20] We have to use signs to express our thoughts, since we first acquire our knowledge from things we perceive with the senses.[21] But as angels do not have bodies or, therefore, know things by sensible signs, they communicate their thoughts in another way. An angel may be said to speak in that it can communicate its thoughts to another angel, but they do not do this with the signs of words. Rather they do this by manifesting their thoughts to another. To manifest is to make clear or to put in the light for others to see. There are two kinds of light: first, corporeal light, by which we see things by the senses of sight, and second, the intelligible light of the mind. Light, St. Thomas says, makes an object actually visible and strengthens the power of sight for seeing. We enlighten others when we communicate to them some truth we know, and similarly angels speak by illuminating the minds of other angels. But speech differs from illumination, St. Thomas says: illumination strengthens the mind for knowing something from above. Thus, only higher angels can illuminate other angels, but lower angels can speak with higher angels, although they cannot illuminate them.[22] Just as we speak with words to manifest the thoughts in our mind, so angels speak by manifesting the conceptions, or inner words, of their minds to other angels. They do this by directing their thoughts to another by their will. Angels do not see into the minds of other angels, but an angel lets another know that it wants to speak to it. As we have already said, angels get their ideas from God. What a good angel sees it sees in the divine Word, but a lower angel does not see all that a higher angel sees. A higher angel sees more clearly and simply. But a lower angel's mind can be illuminated and strengthened to look at something in a higher angel by intuition, for angels do not reason step-by-step discursively as we do in explaining something to another.

How Angels Move

Although angels are not in space, as we are, they are present wherever they are active. Thomas says that they are in a place "by contact of power," where it may be applying its power to a body. He explains how it is possible for angels to be present in the world, although two bodies cannot be in the same place, by saying that there is nothing to stop a spirit from being where there is a body, just as the soul is present in our body. It is common to ridicule medieval thinkers for discussing how many angels can be on the head of a pin, but St. Thomas discusses the more interesting question of whether one angel can be in two places at once. His answer is that it cannot, because an angel is indivisible. Also it can only be in one place at a time because its power is finite. He also looks at the other question, whether two angels can be in one place at the same time, and similarly says no, because it would be like two souls being in one body.[23]

Angels may also move around in the universe from place to place, say from one planet or star to another, as they have wills. St. Thomas thought they might do this in either of two ways: continuously or discontinuously. To move continuously is to pass through all the points of the intervening space; to move discontinuously is to appear first here, in the next instance there, without passing through all the points in between but skipping the space. Although people today dismiss this sort of speculation as unfounded, when St. Thomas says that angels move discontinuously he only anticipates what twentieth-century physicists tell us about the jump of an electron from one orbit to another inside an atom without the transition between the two points being detectable. Asking how long it takes for an angel to move from one place to another is like asking how long it takes to form a thought: it may be instantaneous. Angels move merely by thinking, for their activity is of the intellect, as they are immaterial. An angel can move as quickly as thought, for it has no resistance of body to overcome, but can instantly be where it thinks of, as Shakespeare says of thought:

> For nimble thought can jump both sea and land,
> As soon as think the place where he would be.[24]

The Fall of the Angels

We have already discussed the question, in chapter three, of how evil could arise when everything that God creates is good. The question of how any angel could be evil is all the more difficult, for how could any angel turn away from the good when it sees so much more clearly than we do? It is not as though they choose evil by seeking something that appears good, as human beings do, because they cannot be deceived as we can. As they are intellectual beings, they have open understanding and apprehend the good at the first moment of their existence. How, then, could an angel turn away from the good it sees or lose it? There are two parts to this question. First, were all the angels created good? Second, were they created with final happiness, or was this something they had to choose?

St. Thomas answers the first of these questions by affirming that everything is created good by God. As nothing can be bad by nature, for this would be against its nature, all angels were originally created good.[25] Nothing has a natural inclination to evil, St. Thomas says. As the bad angels were not made bad by nature, they became so by their own will. Evil, St. Thomas says, came from a discord with a higher rule. A double evil is possible for human beings; when our sense appetites are not directed by reason, and when our reason is not directed by divine law and wisdom. The appetite of beasts beneath us are never evil, because they have no higher rule of reason in them to follow. The angels above us can only be bad by not following the rule of divine wisdom.[26] St. Thomas's answer to the first question is that all the angels were made good alike but they varied in the movement of their will.

In his answer to the second question, he draws a distinction between two kinds of happiness: natural and supernatural. We can attain natural happiness by our own powers, but as we cannot gain the second kind of happiness by ourselves, we have to let it be given to us because it is above our nature. This is so because it is a share in God's own eternal beatitude. Thus, we can only have it by grace. As this second kind of happiness is above nature, neither were the angels created in it; they had to choose it. As it was necessary for them to choose it freely, it was also possible for them to lose it by their own choice. St. Thomas thought that they made this choice of will in the first moment of their existence. Every angel moved in the first instance of its existence by an act of will that either merited or forfeited further happiness. It was at this point that a division occurred among the angels, who were all originally created good. Why the angels only had one choice of will, in which they are fixed forever, when we can reverse our previous choice, will be seen below.

We can now see how an angel could have sinned by turning away from God. There are all sorts of sins that angels cannot commit, because they are incorporeal and so do not have passions. Their sins can only be of the intellect. There are two principle sins of the intellect: pride and envy. Pride is not wanting to be under anyone else; envy is grief at another's good or excellence. The bad angels sinned by pride, because they wanted the good of further happiness but they did not want it by receiving it from anyone above them; they wanted to have it as though it were their own. They did not want to be dependent on, or subject to, anyone higher than themselves for supernatural happiness. As they did not want this happiness as though it came from someone above them, their wills were not subject to someone who is above them by nature. Thus, the bad angels sinned and fell by not wanting to receive their ultimate good as a gift from God. As St. Thomas remarks, the fallen angels sought something good, but not in the right way.[27] Their sin lay in wanting to possess their final end of beatitude by their own power rather than by grace. They sinned by wanting to be like God by their own strength, not by God's power.[28]

Nothing can be equal with God, because everything else receives its existence from another, and so shares in existence. Nor did the devil attempt to be equal with God, St. Thomas says. The devil did not seek not to be subject to God absolutely, or he would have ceased to exist, for everything depends for its continued existence on the power of God holding it in existence. Thus, the devil's evil did not lie in the order of nature but of grace, by desiring the end of beatitude by virtue of his own nature and not by grace. Thus, he sought to be like God by seeking something that is proper to God alone: to possess beatitude, "by virtue of his nature and not from the grace of a higher being."[29] Thus, the sin of the devil, and of the angels who followed him, was to want beatitude by his power. He did not sin by seeking evil but by seeking good not in the right order, as coming from the grace of God.

The bad angels are fixed in their first unhappy choice just as the good angels are confirmed in beatitude. They are secure in beatitude, because beatitude is not beatitude as long as there is any possibility or fear of losing it. Final happiness excludes any room for fear. As the beatitude of the good angels is secure, so the bad angels too will not lose their desert. Punishment in the next world is eternal just as eternal life is stable. As the good angels are immovable in their conversion (turning) to God, so the bad angels are immovable in their turning away from God.[30] The angels remain fixed in their first choice for several reasons. It takes time for us to reach the perfection of our nature, since we are corporeal beings, but an angel reaches its perfection straight away with one movement of its will, since it is simple.[31] Thus, its will is not variable like ours. Willing good and evil only belongs to mutable creatures. An angel's will adheres immovably to its first choice, because it apprehends things immovably, not discursively, as it sees clearly into things straight away. St. Thomas says that the will is proportionate to the intellect: the will is immutable like the intellect in angels, because they intuit things directly in their principles. As he remarks, an angel's will is only flexible before its first choice.[32] An angel only has one choice, because it is the step from nature to what is above nature in a single movement.[33] We can see a certain fittingness that the bad angels remain fixed in their choice as the good angels do in theirs. As it is against the idea of perfect happiness that it could be lost, so the bad angels cannot change their pain. As the good angels are confirmed in their first choice, so are the bad angels. As the will of a good angel cannot move to evil, neither can the will of a bad angel move to the good after its first choice. Thus, for St. Thomas, the eternal pain of the bad angels is a matter not only of justice but of the very nature of immaterial beings, who lack a flexible nature like ours because they are simple.

6

The Soul

The soul has almost disappeared from contemporary philosophy and the awareness of most people today. Some philosophers leave out the soul in order to avoid dualism. Many now think that science will be able to explain the mind materially by the working of the brain, without any need of a soul. Even writers who have a great respect for Aquinas largely omit the soul from their account of his thought. Anthony Kenny, for example, using the same tradition of Aristotle as Aquinas, calls the mind "a capacity," which is a good rendering of Aristotle's description of the mind as a power, but he leaves out the soul.[1] Thus, Kenny is reduced to saying that the mind is a capacity of the body, although he also observes that we have some activities of mind and will, such as silent thought, which do not involve any bodily activity.[2] As a capacity is always the capacity of something, the mind cannot be a capacity of the body if it is immaterial, as Kenny thinks it is; so it must be the capacity of something else—the soul. The frequency with which Aquinas mentions the soul throughout his works is enough to let us see that one cannot give a full account of his thought without the soul.

The soul is an integral part of St. Thomas's thought about two areas in which he is held to make a special contribution to philosophy today: the philosophy of mind and moral philosophy. The study of the soul is a prerequisite for ethics, in the opinion of St. Thomas, since the role of the virtues is to direct the powers and appetites of the soul. "We cannot arrive at a perfect knowledge of ethics if we do not understand the powers of the soul," he says.[3] Although John P. O'Callaghan has recently questioned whether Aquinas has a philosophy of mind, as Kenny maintains, I agree with Kenny that what Aquinas says about the intellect is very much what counts as philosophy of mind today in English and American universities. But I agree with O'Callaghan, against Kenny, that the intellect and the will do not form something called the mind over the soul but are powers of the soul according to Aquinas.[4] Rather the mind replaces the soul according to Kenny, as he leaves out the soul, but he thereby falls into the very dualism he is anxious to avoid because he is forced to consider the mind on its own, as was Descartes. Kenny is unable to relate the mind to our other living powers or explain what makes the body living in the first place. For Aquinas, there is a single source of all our vital activities, including thinking: the soul, which gives us our unity.

In modern times, ever since Descartes came to the conclusion that he was a conscious being because he was still aware that he existed even when he supposed that he was not aware of his body, the soul has been equated with consciousness. As he was conscious of himself even when not conscious of his body, he thought that he must be a conscious being, but as this was not his body, it must be something incorporeal—his soul. For Aquinas, on the other hand, as for Aristotle, the soul primarily had not to do with consciousness but with *life*. Indeed, St. Thomas notes that the soul is not just the mind, as Descartes thought, because it includes other powers that cannot be exercised without their bodily organs.[5] Another difference is that to be conscious meant to be self-conscious for Descartes, aware that one exists. As animals do not have this sort of consciousness, he did not think that animals have souls. But for Aristotle and Aquinas, everything living has a soul.

St. Thomas first establishes that the soul is the principle of life. It is not just any principle of life, however, but the primary principle of life. The eye, for example, is the principle of the vital activity of seeing, and the heart of circulating blood. If every principle of life were a body, he says, the eye would be a soul, since it is the principle of vision. But the primary principle of life cannot be a body because if a body were alive just by being a body, every body would be alive. As this is not so, the body is alive because of some principle. St. Thomas calls this principle the "actuality" of the body because it makes a certain kind of body with potential for having life actually living.[6] We can tell that a living body has a primary principle of life, because it is already living before any of the organs of its vital activities appear.

The Form of the Body

Having established that living bodies have a primary principle of life, which is the soul, St. Thomas next shows that the soul is the form of the body. The form of a thing gives it its specific nature. Everything gets its nature from its activities. The activity that is proper to human beings and distinguishes them from all other animals is thinking. Thus, St. Thomas argues that the principle of thinking in each one of us is our form. This is the soul, which is the principle of all our vital activities.

St. Thomas is arguing here on two fronts: against Plato and Averroes (1126–98). Against Plato, Aquinas holds that the soul is united to the body as its form. The soul alone is not the person but is a part of human nature, which includes the body, and only has its perfection in union with the body.[7] Against Averroes, St. Thomas argues that the principle of thinking in us is not some separate or universal mind. He held that the mind is not separate from us in its existence, but only in its operation in that it is not the power of a bodily organ. Aquinas points out that if the mind were separate in its existence, as Averroes held, thinking would not be the activity of this and that individual or anything that I do rather than an external mind does in me. St. Thomas observes that the principle of thinking in me cannot be extraneous, because everyone experiences that it is the same person who thinks as has sensations.[8] There is the same subject of thoughts and sensations because the body has one substantial form.

Not all of Aquinas's contemporaries agreed that a human being has only one substantial form, the rational soul. The chief objection to this view of Aquinas's came from theology, for it seemed that if we only have one substantial form, the soul, then Christ's body had no form when it lay in the tomb. So some said that it had a form of corporeity. The view that we have several forms did not come from Platonists, as is often assumed, but from the Spanish Jewish philosopher Avicebron (Ibn Gabirol), mentioned in the previous chapter. St. Thomas held that, though Christ's soul was separated from his body in death, each remained united to the divine Word. So he denied that Christ was a human being, or therefore the same man, for the time he was in the tomb, because his body did not have its human form, the soul. But Christ was the same person, because body and soul each remained united to divine nature in his person, a Divine person, the Son of God. When he rose again his body and soul were reunited. Thus, he said that Christ's body in the tomb was not the same man but was still the same person, because it was united to the person of the Word.[9]

As the soul is the form of the body, it follows for Aquinas that it is united to the body immediately and not just accidentally, as Plato thought. If the soul were only united to the body accidentally, the body would be alive by something else. But a thing has only one substantial form; this makes a thing be the kind of thing that it is: for instance, a goat, a butterfly, a tree, or a flower. What makes something be the kind of thing that it is cannot be accidental to it. Since the soul is united to the body as its form, it is part of what a human being is by *nature*. Unlike Plato, who thought that the soul is not at home in the body but best freed from it, St. Thomas held that it is natural for the human soul to be embodied. It is only when united to the body that the human soul can exercise the full range of its powers; when it is separated from the body, it only has an incomplete existence until reunited with it. The mind itself is a power of the soul that is the form of the body.

A Subsistent Form

The human soul, however, is a special kind of form for St. Thomas: it is an immaterial and subsistent form. I shall explain how it is both these in turn. St. Thomas presents two arguments for the immateriality of the soul. First, we can know the natures of all bodies but could not do this if the mind were material, because every material body has a determinate nature, which would prevent us from thinking of the natures of all kinds of things, just as liquid poured into a vessel of colored glass seems to have the color of the glass. As we can think of the natures of all kinds of bodies, St. Thomas concludes that the mind does not share the material nature of any one of them.[10]

Second, the mind is immaterial because we can think of things in an immaterial way: that is, not just as they exist in matter with their individual characteristics, but also generally. Nothing is general in its material existence; rather every material thing is individual and particular in its own existence. So, if I can think of material things, like horses, generally, this is not as they exist in matter, but immaterially. We could not think of things in an immaterial way unless the mind was immaterial.

> From knowing the universal natures of things, the human soul perceives that the likeness by which it thinks of something is immaterial; otherwise it would be individual and this would not lead to general knowledge of things.[11]

Thus, we have immaterial knowledge of material things. If the mind were material, St. Thomas says, it would only know things individually, as the senses do. To know an individual stone and to know it just as stone in general differ from one another. To know a stone in the second way is to have the general idea, or concept, of what stone is.[12] St. Thomas held that we get our general concepts of material things by abstracting them from sense impressions. Plato held that the forms of things exist immaterially on their own, but Aristotle and Aquinas believed that we have to abstract them from matter; they are not abstract in reality, as Plato held, but only in the mind.

Although talk of abstracting ideas is scorned at present, it can be found in Gottlob Frege (1848–1925), the father of modern linguistic philosophy. Frege says that when I disregard the properties that distinguish the items of a set of things, I get a concept under which they come. For example, when I overlook the difference in color of fur of a group of cats or the features that distinguish leopards from cheetahs, I get the concept of cat. Frege says that "the concept has been gained by abstraction."[13] This agreement of Frege with Aquinas should render Aquinas's theory of abstracting ideas quite acceptable today.

St. Thomas adopted Aristotle's theory that we abstract our concepts by the power of the active intellect, which both compare with a light. We then receive the ideas that the active intellect makes in the receptive intellect. Aquinas does not call it the receptive but "possible" intellect because it begins as a *tabula rasa*, and we have to acquire our ideas; the mind is not already equipped with innate ideas, as Plato thought. But, as Kenny points out, the active and possible intellects are not two intellects; rather they are two powers of one and the same intellect. Moreover, Aristotle and Aquinas thought that this is our own intellect, or mind, not some separate universal mind acting in us, as Avicenna and Averroes thought. They thought this was the correct interpretation of Aristotle when he says that the intellect is something "separate."[14] But Aquinas argues against their interpretation that the context makes it clear that Aristotle did not mean that our intellect is separate in its existence—it is separate only in its activity, being a power that is not of the body.[15] Aquinas also notes that you cannot act through something that is separate from you in its existence, if it is to be your thinking.[16]

St. Thomas thought that thinking of things in an immaterial way is not itself the activity of a corporeal organ, such as the brain. St. Thomas, however, thought that we need the brain for thinking, because we cannot think of things without turning to images or sense-impressions (*phantasmata*, as he calls them).[17] The intellect needs sense-impressions, he says, as the eye needs colors to see things.[18] We cannot think of things without turning to images, because natures only have actual existence in individuals, which we apprehend with the senses. The concept or general idea of a lion, for example, contains the definition of a lion. The definition gives its nature. The nature of a lion does not exist on its own as the Form or Idea of a lion, as Plato held, but only in bodily lions. Thus, we do not get our idea of a lion by beholding the Idea of a lion but from the sense-impressions of individual lions we have seen (or from pictures of them). We think of things in images just as natures only have actual existence in individuals, which we apprehend with the senses. David Hume, for instance, said that I never think of anything without having a mental image of it. However abstract Aquinas may seem to be, he never forgot that we need the senses of the body for our way of knowing things. All knowledge (*cognitio*) takes its being from the senses, he frequently says. We need the brain for supplying the sense-data, or information, on which we think. But abstracting our general ideas from the sense-impressions of things is not the work of the brain but of the intellect. Thus, the human soul has an activity that is not the activity of a corporeal organ.

What has an independent activity, that is, one not involving a bodily organ, also has an independent existence: that is, does not depend on the body for its existence. From this St. Thomas concludes that the human soul is also a *subsistent* form, for nothing can work by itself unless it subsists, that is, exists in its own right, so to speak. Only human souls are subsistent: the souls of other animals are not subsistent like this because the sensitive soul has no activity that is not also the activity of a bodily organ. Thus, the souls of animals are not immortal, because they are altogether tied to their bodies and so perish with them.[19]

As the human soul is the form of the body and it is subsistent, it is a subsistent form. This was a development by Aquinas of Aristotle's theory of the soul, for Aristotle says nothing about its being a subsistent form. Nor, so far as I have been able to discover, does St. Thomas's master, St. Albert the Great, say that the human soul is subsistent. This insight of Aquinas's is the keystone of his demonstration that the human soul is immortal.

Immortality

Strictly speaking, St. Thomas does not say in the *Summa* that the soul is immortal but incorruptible, although elsewhere he frequently calls it immortal. It will suffice here to give just three of his arguments for the immortality of the soul. First, as it is immaterial, it has no quantity, so it is indivisible.[20] Second, a thing ceases to exist when it loses its form, but something that can subsist just as a form (when separated from the body) cannot be separated from itself.[21] Third, what is corrupted is the composite whole of body and soul, but this does not prevent a part from remaining in existence.[22] A similar point was made by the Cambridge philosopher John Ellis McTaggart (1866–1925), who remarked that natural science supports rather than disproves the idea of immortality, since it only tells us about the destruction of compounds. Nothing is annihilated in nature, but only combinations of units cease to exist.[23] Aquinas also notes that the soul does not corrupt because there is no contrariety in the mind as in the senses. A thing can be too bright or too hot or too cold for the senses and damage them; but the thought of light does not exclude the thought of dark in the mind, and the mind can never see a thing too clearly.[24]

For St. Thomas the incorruptibility of the human soul goes with its immediate creation by God. He argues that since the human soul surpasses the capacity of matter in the way that it also knows things immaterially, it cannot be drawn from matter.[25] He notes that Aristotle, too, discerned that the mind (*nous*) must "come in from outside," because it is not the power of a bodily organ and so cannot be transmitted with the seed by physical generation.[26] To Aquinas it was clear that the principle of thinking in human beings transcends matter, for it has an activity in which no bodily organ shares, namely, thinking of things in an immaterial and general way. As the human soul is immaterial, it cannot be generated by the parents but is caused by a creative act of God.[27] It is created because it is immaterial and so made out of nothing. St. Thomas also saw evidence for the creation of the soul in the Gospel of St. John 1:9, where it says that it is the Word "who enlightens everyone coming into the world." Aquinas takes "coming into the world" with "everyone" and not, as mostly today, with the Word ("coming" immediately follows everyone, not the Word, in the Greek). He asks how everyone comes *into* the world and says that this is not by our corporeal but intellectual nature. If it were by our corporeal nature, it would say "*from* the world," not into the world. In support of his view, St. Thomas then quotes *Qoholet* 12:7: "the spirit returns to God who gave it." The Word enlightens everyone who comes into the world, because all light of the mind derives from God.[28]

St. Thomas observes that if the soul were not created, it would not be in the image of God. The image of God lies in a power of the soul, not in its essence, because the soul includes other powers besides the mind.[29] The power of intelligence is like a stamp of the divine light impressed in us: "The light of your face is marked upon us" (Ps 4:6).[30]

So far I have highlighted three points of St. Thomas's doctrine of the soul: it is the form of the body, it is immaterial, and it is immortal. Moreover, as the soul is immaterial, it comes directly from God. I shall now consider three main difficulties of St. Thomas's doctrine, which arise from each of these points in turn.

First, how is the soul united to the body as its form when thinking is not a power of the body? There have been two ways of getting round this difficulty. One is to say that the mind is material like the body. The other is to say that the intellect does not belong to the individual human being but is a separate, universal intellect acting in everyone. As we have seen, the second way was taken by the Arab philosophers Avicenna and Averroes. A version of it can still be met today, even among natural scientists. The physicist Erwin Schrödinger, for example, thought that we all share in one consciousness because each person only experiences consciousness in the singular, and we each have a little patch on it where our ideas are not part of a common outlook.

Although thinking is not the activity of a bodily organ, the soul can still be the form of the body because it has other powers that actualize organs of the body. Thus, the soul can be the form of the body, although its highest power is not the function of a bodily part. In this way St. Thomas is able to show that it is not just a mind that thinks, as Descartes thought, but the whole person, because the mind is a power of the soul and the soul is united to the whole human being as his or her form. For Descartes, it seems that a mind rather than a human being thinks, for he isolates the mind from the body. But by making the mind a power of the soul and holding that the soul is united to a human being as his or her form, St. Thomas shows that it is the whole person who thinks. Thus, Aquinas is fully in accord with philosophers of the twentieth century who demand that a human being thinks, not just a mind.

The human soul transcends the body by its capacity to think of things in an immaterial way, but it is not separate in its existence. Body and soul share one existence, which Aquinas calls "the soul's act of existence," because the soul gives the body its existence. The soul is not a power of the body but the actuality of the body, which makes it alive. As the soul is not a power, it cannot be identical with its powers.

This helps us see why the soul is not its powers but its powers are "rooted" in its essence.[31] Many powers of the soul are of something joint: sensation, for example, also requires the body. But all the powers, including thinking and understanding, are united in one principle. The soul is the cause of the powers, which flow from it. Body and soul are united, because the soul alone is not the subject of all its powers, but the subject of many of its powers is something joint, the soul with the body, for many of these powers can only be exercised with corporeal organs.[32] As the soul is not identical with its powers, the soul cannot just be the sum of the properties of a living body, as it is sometimes said to be today. If all that we meant by the soul were the properties that make a body living, thought too would be a property of matter. St. Thomas explicitly says that the powers are properties of the soul, not of the body.[33] He defines a power as a principle of action.

The second difficulty is, how can the soul be the form of the body when it is something subsistent? St. Thomas tackles this question in two parts in his *Quaestiones de Anima*, q.1. He first argues that the soul is subsistent, because it has an independent activity in which the body does not share. He then shows that it is the form, because it is that by which a body is a living one. As the human soul is subsistent and a form, it is a subsistent form. This point has been well expressed by Victor Brezik: either forms depend on matter and are not subsistent, or they are independent of matter and are subsistent. Forms that depend on matter have no activity of their own, but the human soul has an activity that is not that of a bodily organ, namely thinking, and so is subsistent.[34]

At this point, one might think that, because the soul is subsistent, Aquinas runs into dualism by making us consist of two substances, for the body is a substance, too. Aquinas explains that something can be subsistent in two ways: either as a hand or foot may be called a subsistent thing or as something that has a complete nature. The soul is not subsistent in this second way, he says, because it is not the whole human being. Only the composite whole of body and soul together is subsistent in the second way. The soul is a subsistent thing in the first way, because it does not have the complete nature of a human being; rather it completes a human being.[35] To make clearer the unity of body and soul, I would add the following two points. First, a hand or foot is not a subsistent thing on its own but only as part of a living body; neither has actions of its own when severed from the body. Second, it is assumed that the body is a substance, but a body is not a living substance without its soul. Thus, there is a *substantial union* of body and soul, so that they make *one* substance, although the soul is something subsistent.

The soul is united to every part of the body, because it gives existence to the whole body. It is whole in every part of the body in its essence, St. Thomas says, but not in its powers, because its powers are exercised by different parts of the body.[36]

The soul is united to the body as its form but is also raised above the body by its power to think of things in an immaterial way. Its existence is raised above the body because it has an activity that is not a power of the body. As St. Thomas observes, the human soul is not totally immersed in matter on account of its nobility.[37] The human soul seems to be raised above the body because we can reflect on our actions and thinking, which is from above. St. Thomas thought that self-reflection shows that the human soul is immaterial, for he notes that when we think, we also think of our thinking, but no material organ can do this.[38] For example, the eye sees, but it does not see or know that it sees. Thus, St. Thomas sees human beings as having a special position in creation, being the meeting point between the purely immaterial and the material.

> Inasmuch as the soul has an activity transcending the material it is raised above the body and is not dependent on it. But inasmuch as it is made to acquire immaterial knowledge from material things it is not complete in its nature apart from union with the body. Thus a human being stands on the border [in confinio] between corporeal and separate substances.[39]

Separate substances for Aquinas, as mentioned in the previous chapter, are angels and human souls when separated for the body.

The third difficulty of St. Thomas's account of the soul that I want to consider here arises from the immortality of the soul. How can the soul remain individual after it is separated from the body by death when forms are individuated by being in different lumps of matter? It would seem that when the soul is no longer in the body, it loses its individuality and identity. St. Thomas resolves this difficulty by resorting to the idea of existence: the soul retains its individuality because it continues with the same existence as it had previously in the body, and the existence of each soul is the existence of having been in just this particular body. "Through acquiring the individual existence of this body it always remains individual in its existence."[40] As the human soul does not perish with the body, because it is subsistent, so neither does its individuality, which it acquired by being in this one body. Peter Geach points out that the individuation of the soul by its particular body is not merely retrospective but also prospective, because the soul retains the capacity to be reunited with its body.[41] "Thus the human soul," St. Thomas says, "remains in its existence when it has been separated from the body, having a natural aptitude and inclination for union with the body."[42] This is because the soul is meant by nature to be joined to the body. When the body is destroyed, the soul remains in its existence but not in the completion of its nature. St. Thomas was quite prepared to draw the consequence of his view that the soul by itself is not the human being and so denied that the separated soul is a human person, for the reason that it does not have the complete nature of the human species.[43] More about the soul's reunion with its body will be said on the Resurrection in chapter twelve.

Although it is common at present to call St. Thomas a dualist, because he says that the human soul is subsistent, in truth his account of the soul provides an antidote to the dualist view of human beings that we find in Plato and Descartes. What I am is not just my soul, because whatever is the human being must have the complete activities of a human being, St. Thomas says. One of these is sensation, which requires a body.[44] We are a unity of body and soul, because there is a single principle of all our vital activities: that by which we think is also that by which we live and move. This was not so for Descartes, who said that the body can carry on all its operations that do not depend on the will, independently of the soul. When the soul is left out, we cease to understand the unity of a human being, for the body gets its unity from its form, which makes it alive. Leaving out the soul may seem to preserve the unity of a human being, but it fails to explain why the body is a living one. We have already seen that Anthony Kenny is unable to show what the mind is a capacity of when it is immaterial, because he leaves out the linchpin, so to speak, of the whole explanation of the human being.

When we patiently examine St. Thomas's doctrine of the soul, we find that it is not necessary to dispense with the soul in order to avoid dualism. On the contrary, the soul is the very thing that explains the unity of the human being. The body has no unity without that which makes it alive, its principle of life, but visibly falls apart when the soul departs. To leave out the soul is to discard that in which we are made in the image of God. For this image comes not from matter below by the process of evolution but directly from God above as the stamp of our Maker impressed in us. I conclude, then, that the soul and the mind have the same unity in the thought of St. Thomas as those who leave out the soul think a human being has. We next go on to consider an area in which we particularly see that there is a unity of body and soul—in the emotions.

7

The Emotions

A valuable but little studied part of St. Thomas's thought is his treatise on the emotions in the first part of the second part of the *Summa*, questions 22–49. It is also one of his longest and most intricate treatises on a single topic. These questions give us the psychology of St. Thomas, in the true sense of the word "psychology," which literally means "the study of the soul." Much psychology done today makes no reference to the soul. Also modern psychology is more concerned with the morbid and exceptional whereas the psychology of St. Thomas is chiefly about the normal reactions of human beings to everyday things. St. Thomas also provides firm guiding principles for psychology, because his is based on the powers of the soul, and thus on the human nature of everyone. In these questions we also discover the deep and gentle humanity of St. Thomas, who could be as understanding of human nature as he was penetrating and lofty in abstract thought. We also find in them some of his best remarks about prayer, love, and friendship, for St. Thomas saw life as a whole, in which everything is explained and united by certain underlying principles. His psychology is based on

Aristotle, who only provides us with a sketch of the emotions. What St. Thomas gives us is something immensely more refined, as he was able to draw on the wisdom of several centuries of Christian thinkers, from East and West.

St. Thomas himself does not use the word "emotion" but talks about the passions. The Latin *passio* is an exact equivalent for Aristotle's *pathos*, which suggests being affected by something. Passion for us today, however, has come to mean something rather narrower: the word now usually suggests a strong or violent emotion of love or anger. A passion for St. Thomas is often something calmer and broader than this. Thus, I shall mostly translate St. Thomas's *passio* as "emotion." This word has the advantage of showing that we have passions, or emotions, because one thing is moved by another: the body is moved by the soul. A movement of the soul causes a change in the body. For example, people turn white with fear, are visibly angry, and can be radiant with joy. "Since the soul naturally moves the body, a spiritual movement of the soul is naturally the cause of an alteration of the body."[1] As St. Thomas observes, "A vestige of the heart most shines in the face, tongue and the eyes."[2]

The soul has four powers: two of these are rational, and two are irrational. The rational powers of the soul are reason and will; the irrational powers are the two sensitive appetites: the concupiscible, or desiring, and the irascible appetites. We have emotions because we have a sensitive nature. Every animal is equipped with the desiring and irascible appetites, so that it first seeks the good things that it needs to preserve its life and can then overcome any obstacles it meets in seeking the good it needs. This is with the irascible appetite. As St. Thomas observes, the natural appetite tends first to conserve nature and then to destroy what is harmful. There is also an appetite of the rational part of our nature: this is the will. The emotions, then, are movements of our sensitive appetites when we apprehend things as good or evil.

For his definition of an emotion, St. Thomas adopts the one of St. John Damascene, an Eastern father: an emotion is "a movement of the appetite felt as a result of the impression of something good or evil."[3] St. Thomas remarks that there have been two views about the emotions. The Stoics thought that they were bad; the Stoics' aim was to achieve a state of invulnerability (*apatheia*, literally "of not feeling"), so that one is affected neither by well-being and success nor by adversity. St. Thomas thought that this was to be less than fully human, since we have a sensitive nature and so have emotions by nature. Instead he favored the view of Aristotle and the Peripatetics that the passions are good when they are moderate, and only bad when they exceed the moderation of reason.[4] St. Thomas even regarded the experience of emotions as part of our moral perfection, because controlling the movements of our sensitive appetites by reason belongs to virtue. Moral virtue does not exclude emotion, in St. Thomas's view, but includes it. Indeed he thought that we cannot have virtue without emotion, because we find joy in acting well and have sorrow about doing wrong.[5] Contrary to the Stoics, and probably to many people today, St. Thomas thought that there is nothing intrinsically bad about the emotions: in themselves they are neutral. They are only good or bad as they come under reason and the command of the will. They are good or bad as they are voluntary, and they are voluntary as they are commanded or prohibited by the will.[6] St. Thomas shared Aristotle's view that the sensitive appetites are not altogether irrational, as Plato thought, but share in reason when they obey it. If our lower sensitive appetites could not share in reason, he thought, sadness would arise as they would resist reason and reason would be moved by violence.[7] Whether emotions are good or bad depends on whether they are in accord or discord with reason.[8] When they are not directed by reason, they cause disturbances (*perturbationes*), St. Thomas notes.[9]

As there are two sensitive appetites, the desiring and the irascible, and they have two objects, good and evil, there are four principle emotions: joy and sorrow, hope and fear. St. Thomas says that they are four in number because they concern seeking good and fleeing from evil either as these are present or still future. The object of joy is present good, and of hope is future good. Likewise, the object of sorrow is present evil, and of fear is of evil that lies ahead. We either move away from or toward what lies ahead of us—so fear flees from future evil and hope strains toward future good. The irascible appetite only concerns things as they are difficult to obtain or avoid; we do not hope to get something we are bound to get or fear something that is easy to overcome. So fear and hope have to do with the "arduous," St. Thomas says. He notes that the objects of the desiring appetite are good and evil, simply speaking; but the objects of the irascible appetite is something difficult or arduous. The emotions of the desiring appetite, joy and sorrow, rest in present good or evil; those of the irascible appetite move toward or away from their objects. As the end of all motion is rest, the emotions of the irascible appetite are directed toward those of the desiring appetite. "Thus all of the emotions of the irascible terminate in the emotions of the concupiscible. And accordingly, joy and sorrow, which are in the concupiscible appetite, follow on the emotions of the irascible."[10] Thus, hope turns into joy and fear into sorrow or pain.

The principle emotions are also four in number because there is a double opposition: of good and evil and of moving toward (*accessus*) or away from (*recessus*).[11] Moving toward and away from may be compared to the motion of the tides: the sea comes up to us on the beach at high tide and recedes from us when the tide turns. When good recedes from us, it seems as though our life is at a low ebb. Thus, hope is the opposite of fear: the one moves toward the good; the other away from evil.

St. Thomas also notes that, like the positive and negative forces of a magnet, good attracts and evil repels us. Things are good because they agree with our nature, he says, and evil because they do not suit it. It is reason that apprehends things as good or evil; the imagination finds things pleasant or painful. When St. Thomas uses the word "evil" (*malum*), he often does not mean it in the moral sense but as what is bad for something: thus arsenic is an evil for us because it disagrees with the chemistry of our body, although it is neutral in itself (a tiny trace is good for us as it is part of our nature). We naturally seek things we find agreeable and turn away from what is repugnant. Thus, the spring of all action, St. Thomas says, is either love of the good that attracts us or hate of the evil that repels us.

To St. John Damascene's definition of emotion as a movement of the sensitive appetite, Aquinas joins Aristotle's theory of motion in the *Physics*. Aristotle notes that all motion has three phases: a beginning, a middle, and an end. It is from one point, or term, to another: something gets from where it begins to the end by moving in between. All movement has a beginning.

The beginning is an inclination. An inclination is to something good. St. Thomas uses the nature of motion to show us that, as there are three phases of movement, two appetites and two kinds of object, good and evil, so the four principle emotions yield us eleven emotions. It is eleven rather than twelve, because one of them, anger, for reasons that we shall see, has no contrary. All the emotions of the concupiscible appetite move either toward the good or away from evil (nothing moves away from the good or seeks the evil). We have an inclination for what is good; this is love, which becomes desire as we move toward the good, and comes to rest in joy when we obtain the good object. For example, I have an inclination toward sparkling mineral water, I move toward it with desire, and I come to rest in the enjoyment of it when it reaches my throat. Hate, on the other hand, moves away from evil in flight, as it detests it, but ends in sorrow when we come to rest in evil.

We have already noted that there are two kinds of contraries among the emotions: of good and evil, and of moving toward and away from things, which St. Thomas calls *accessus* and *recessus*. Thus, the emotions come in pairs. Moving toward and receding from the good in the irascible appetite gives us hope and despair. We do not just despair about evils; we can also despair about good things, such as salvation, when we think they are impossible to attain.[12] Likewise, moving toward and away from evil gives us audacity (boldness) and fear. When we have in sight the end of our labors and difficulties, we are encouraged to go on to grasp the reward. Thus, hope turns to audacity. For instance, when the summit is in view, a mountaineer is emboldened to tackle the remaining dangers with fresh heart. But when we see the good we hope for recede, hope turns to despair. The object of hope is something good as possible to attain. But fear can turn either way: to despair when there is no more hope of escaping an evil, or to daring and anger when timid persons are frustrated by their lack of power and see themselves driven into a corner; then they turn round and attack what oppresses them with unexpected force. Our reaction to evil that lies on top of us is anger, which has no contrary because, if it rested in evil, it would be sorrow. Anger, however, does not rest in evil or flee from it but *attacks* it.[13] There is also no contrary of anger, because there is no emotion of the irascible appetite for present good, only of present evil (attacking it, not resting in it).[14] Thus, we get the following pairs of contrary emotions under the desiring appetite: love and hate, desire and detestation, joy and sorrow. And under the irascible appetite: hope and despair, audacity and fear, and anger, which has no contrary. This gives us the following table of emotions for concupiscible and irascible appetites:

Appetite	CONCUPISCIBLE		IRASCIBLE	
Object	Good	Evil	Good	Evil
Emotion	love	hate	HOPE	FEAR
	desire	detestation	despair	audacity
	JOY	SORROW		anger

Note: The four primary emotions are in capital letters

St. Thomas observes that all our emotions either move toward something (flight from evil is movement toward the good) or rest in something, good or evil. As the spring of all our actions is either love or hate, and only the emotions of the desiring appetite come to rest, for those of the irascible appetite are always in motion toward good or away from evil, all our actions begin with love or hate, and end in joy or sorrow. Having thus sketched the relation of the emotions to one another, I shall now consider more closely four of them, which seem to me especially interesting: love and joy, sorrow and anger.

Love

St. Thomas reduces, that is, leads back, all the emotions to love. He gives us two definitions of love: a fitting of the appetite to something good and being pleased with the good.[15] Love is the spring of all the emotions, because we are moved to act by an end, and only the good can be an end (we do not seek evil). Love is like natural gravity, St. Thomas says: we tend to move toward what we love. Love obviously causes desire. Love is also the cause of sorrow, because sorrow arises from the loss of what we love: for instance, a possession or a friend. Nonetheless, he says that sorrow is caused more by present evil than loss of the good we love.[16] Love also causes hate, because we hate what is opposed to our good. Hate, however, seems not always to be of evil, for some people hate the truth and want to suppress it.[17] When people hate the good, it is because it gets in the way of what they, wrongly, perceive to be their good or of their own wicked plans. Although it seems that we cannot always lead hate back to love, because sometimes hate appears to be a stronger emotion than love, this is because its expression is stronger, St. Thomas says. Hate is more apparent in its expression, because it is of its nature a less peaceful emotion. Second, in some circumstances, people seem to be more moved by hate of evil than love of good; for instance, most criminals would rather be deprived of their freedom for a long time in prison than suffer shortly but sharply by being beaten with the birch. Even here, St. Thomas says, we shun pain because we first love the good of our existence, and all pain, leading up to the greatest pain of death itself, is opposed to our well-being.[18] Removing pain, which is a flight from evil, springs from love because it is directed to enjoying something: a toothache prevents us from enjoying anything. Thus, love is prior to hate. Because we love what is agreeable and hate what is repugnant or harmful, St. Thomas describes love as a *consonance* and hate as a *dissonance*.[19]

Love is also the cause of the emotions of the irascible appetite. The nearest of these to love is hope, because it is directed to the good. The others can then be led back to love as they go back to hope. Hope is the cause of fear, as flight from evil is at the same time movement to the good—for example, from danger to safety. We fear the loss of what we love or hope to attain. Fears are often caused by love, St. Thomas remarks.[20] Hope turns into daring, or audacity, as we have already seen, and anger follows when we meet with resistance that persists. For example, when I am trying to thread a needle, first my irascible appetite is aroused to overcome a slight difficulty, and when the resistance of the thread to the needle persists, impatience or anger ensues.

As all the emotions can be led back to love in this way, love is the root of all the emotions, because only an emotion of the desiring appetite can rest in the end. Emotions of the irascible appetite either tend toward some good ahead (hope) or flee from evil (fear) or confront it (audacity and anger), but evil is not an end itself. As all the emotions spring from love, they all have a unity when ordered by love.[21]

Love is a unifying force, a *vis unitiva*, a phrase from Pseudo-Dionysius that St. Thomas likes to repeat. St. Thomas also explains why we experience loving people as warm and unloving people as cold. Love is warm because when things become warm they fuse together. Conversely, lack of love appears cold because cold things do not easily mix. As things contract when they become cold, unloving people do not go out to others.[22]

An effect of love is union.[23] Love causes union, because one of its effects is that the lover is in the beloved. This is well described for us in Sir Philip Sidney's poem "The Bargain":

My true love hath my heart, and I have his,
By just exchange, one for the other given . . .
His heart in me keeps me and him in one,
My heart in him his thoughts and senses guides;
He loves my heart, for once it was his own,
I cherish his, because in me it bides.

One way the beloved is in the lover, St. Thomas says, is that the lover counts the joys and sorrows of the beloved as his or her own. Friends have joy or sorrow about the same things. They are also in each other, because the love of friendship is reciprocal; it is a *radamatio* (a love in return).[24] The lover is in the beloved because he or she is not content with a merely superficial knowledge but wants to know the other more interiorly.

We are united with others either by presence to them or by affection. Affection remains even when friends are separated by distance. When the object of our love is present, the result is joy. But when the object is absent, either of two emotions can arise: desire or longing for what one loves, or sorrow at not possessing it. Thus, love causes sorrow when a friend is absent. This double effect of love resulting in joy or sorrow may sometimes be combined, as we find when St. Paul writes: "I long day and night to see you, remembering you with tears, so that I may be filled with joy" (2 Tm 1:4). The longing, which is accompanied here by some sorrow, will lead to joy on seeing Timothy again.

Joy

We distinguish between joy and pleasure; joy is of the mind, pleasure of the senses. Animals have pleasure but not joy. Joy is an emotion of the *interior* appetite, St. Thomas says. Only pleasure that comes with the interior apprehension of the mind also brings joy.[25] Joy comes from pleasure that goes with reason.[26] Thus, joy, strictly speaking, is an emotion of the intellectual rather than sensitive appetite.

Joy is the one emotion that we share with God and the good angels, although it is not an emotion in them, for they are not moved as we are, since they are incorporeal. The highest pleasure, Aristotle says, lies in the exercise of wisdom, which is contemplation or consideration of the truth for its own sake.[27] The highest joy we can have is to contemplate God. Thus, contemplation is a source of joy that begins in this life, St. Thomas says, but will only be complete in eternity.[28] Contemplation brings joy, because we derive more pleasure from what we know with the mind than with the senses. We derive greater pleasure from the things of the mind than from the senses, because the mind reflects on its activity. We would rather be without sight than understanding, St. Thomas remarks. The knowledge of the mind is more interior, as the senses only know the outside of things but the mind can penetrate beyond the appearances and surface of a thing to its essence. The mind has pleasure in acquiring knowledge and reflecting on it. Wonder too is a source of delight when we discover something new. Thus, we receive joy from the two activities of inquiry (*inquisitio*) and contemplation.[29] Aristotle remarks that God rejoices in a single activity, which is the contemplation of himself, the highest and most lovable good.[30]

We also delight in virtuous *activity*—for example, in helping others by acts of kindness and mercy—because we regard the good of another as our own on account of the love that regards a friend as another self.[31] Any activity that comes easily and naturally brings us pleasure. No one gets much pleasure from playing the piano, for example, unless he or she can do it with a certain ease.

One indication that animals only experience pleasure but not joy is that they cannot smile. Only happy people can smile; unhappy people can laugh but not easily smile. We laugh at something external, but happiness comes from an interior state or attitude. Joy differs from pleasure, because pleasure turns to sorrow when it is not moderated, but joy knows no end. We talk of someone's joy being "unbounded." But pleasure of the senses leads to sadness when unchecked, and sad people in turn seek pleasure of the senses as a flight from what oppresses their mind, because it temporarily distracts them from thinking about their pain.[32] Drinking alcohol brings pleasure until sorrow sets in when we begin to lose the use of reason.[33]

Pleasure turns to sorrow, because too much activity of the senses causes weariness and strain. Excessive activity also causes pain, because it is opposed to the balance and well being of our powers. With too much activity of the senses pleasure turns into boredom (*taedium*).[34] Thus, we can at times lose interest in what normally holds our attention, because the brain and imagination get tired. The remedy for the sorrow that comes from overwork is games and rest, St. Thomas recommends.[35] But there is no contrary to the joy of the mind. Although joy of the mind is greater than the pleasure of the senses, most people seek the latter because it is more immediate and quicker to attain. Bodily pleasures are stronger because they have contraries, but the delights of the mind have no contrary sorrows and so lack contrast.

The greatest pleasure of the senses comes from the sense of touch, which is spread over the whole body. Touch is the fundamental and most deeply seated sense, because it is concerned with what preserves our life.[36] The other senses only have a single organ or pair of organs. Animals mostly get pleasure from the sense of touch, but we get it from the other senses too, especially from those of sight and hearing, because they are closest to the mind. Many of our words for understanding, like "insight," "seeing the reason" and so on, are drawn from an analogy with the sense of sight. Sight and hearing are the most "knowing" senses, St. Thomas remarks.[37] It is especially with these two that we apprehend and regard beauty. Animals do not have a sense of beauty, which goes with the intellect, because it depends on the faculty to discern form, proportion, and consonance in things. But with us at times, as when listening to some music, the experience of art does not just bring pleasure but borders on joy.

Sorrow

The opposite of joy is sorrow. One difference between joy and sorrow is that we try to get rid of sorrow but not of joy. There are two kinds of sorrow: sadness (*tristitia*) and pain (*dolor*). As joy is interior pleasure, so sadness is interior sorrow. Sadness is in the mind and psychological; pain is physical. Pain differs from sorrow in that it belongs to the sense of touch; sorrow can accompany the other senses. When I bite my tongue or the light is too bright for my eyes, I have pain. But the sight of something disagreeable or distressing causes sorrow in me. Pain arises from division and conflict in us—in other words from a lack of unity.[38] These cause pain because we desire unity in ourselves and with others. The unity of a thing is its good because something exists as it is one, as we have already noted in chapter three. A clock, for example, only exists as a clock as long as its parts are united and make one thing. This is even more so with living creatures. Something is only completely good when all its powers and parts are in harmony and unison. When they are in harmony, it functions at its best. Everything seeks unity as it seeks its good, which is to exist as one being. Pain and sorrow arise from being impatient of, literally not suffering, division and disintegration. We naturally do not suffer or tolerate disunity. Love itself, as we have already noted, is an appetite for unity. Thus, the desire for unity causes sorrow as it seeks to be separated from harm. Any kind of detachment from things we love, which is a form of separation, also causes sorrow, even when we willingly renounce the pleasure of lower things for the sake of a higher or spiritual good. This is also why abandoning some form of addiction is painful.

Pain and sorrow take away all pleasure, because attention is first drawn to what is contrary to our good and gets in the way of our well-being.[39] Great pleasure or pain prevents us from thinking, St. Thomas observes, because thought involves the use of the imagination, which is absorbed by pleasure or pain, as all the powers of the soul are rooted in its essence.[40] Anything that is contrary to the inclination of the appetite saddens us (is *contristans*). St. Thomas notes that physical pain, like a toothache, hinders contemplation more than interior pain or sadness.[41]

Interior pain, however, can be greater than physical pain, because evil is more known by interior apprehension than by the senses.[42] Thus, St. Thomas says that Christ suffered the greatest pain of all on the cross not only because his body was more sensitive as he was perfect but also because he had a much clearer apprehension of the wrong being done to him and the evil of the sin.

Aquinas follows the authority of Nemesius of Emesa, who flourished AD 390–400, and St. John Damascene in naming four kinds of sorrow: anxiety, torpor, pity, and envy.[43]

Anxiety comes from the Latin word *angustiae*, which means a narrow pass, confined place, or strait. The German word *Angst* derives directly from *angustiae*. Thus, anxiety arises when we perceive ourselves to be in a strait with no way out of a difficulty, like repaying a debt or meeting expectations in work. Pain is caused by something present; anxiety is about the future. As the route of escape from some difficulty is blocked and someone is hemmed in, so one of the effects of anxiety is to restrict the movement of the body.[44] A tennis player may not perform so well when carrying a great sorrow or worry. Joy and hope, on the other hand, cause us to dilate and expand. Sadness weighs down the body, because it hinders the will from enjoying anything. And sorrow distresses our nature, because it impedes movement toward the good.[45] It is like a weight that holds down the body and thus restricts its easy movement. When anxiety does this, it leads to torpor, which is slowness of movement. In extreme sorrow, this results in speechlessness, an inability to move the mouth and tongue. When sorrow weighs us down, it affects our health and we commonly feel "run down."[46] Anxiety eventually leads to despair, when we see no more hope of escaping an evil or difficulty. When there is no more motive for acting, because the situation seems hopeless, despair leads to inactivity. Thus, anxiety produces torpor.

Torpor weighs down the body as anxiety weighs down the mind. Thus, as just said, anxiety makes a person silent. Sorrow is of its nature opposed to the vital movement of the body, because it opposes appetite.[47] Torpor is the accidie, or *akedia*, described by John Cassian (ca. 360–435) in his *Conferences*. Another result of anxiety is the loss of appetite.

Pity (*misericordia*) is the sorrow we feel for another's evil as though it were our own. Thus, pity is compassion, which means to share someone's suffering.

Envy is the opposite of pity: it is sorrow at another's good, either because someone else's good fortune gets in the way of the good you seek for yourself or because it means the loss of some good by yourself. We envy someone who receives the praise or attention we hoped to receive ourselves. Iago, for example, envied Cassio because Othello preferred him to Iago as his lieutenant. Whatever prevents us from attaining a good we desire causes sorrow, because we experience being deprived of good as an evil. Envy sometimes turns to hate so that we seek to destroy someone who enjoys a good we cannot have for ourselves.[48] Thus, many murders are crimes of passion, where the lover kills the loved one out of envy of another who has gained his or her love in the lover's place. Envy and pity are both forms of sadness, because they concern one's own evil either as another's evil is felt to be one's own or as the loss of some good is one's evil. Pity is sorrow for another's adversity; envy sorrow for another's prosperity. Pity is always a good emotion, St. Thomas says; envy is always bad.

The opposite of envy is repentance, because it is sorrow about the evil one has done oneself rather than about the good of another. One might think that repentance would count as a fifth of these sorrows, but St. Thomas discounts it because it is about one's own evil, whereas the above four kinds of sorrow concern another's evil outside oneself. But elsewhere St. Thomas makes various observations about repentance: it is a good form of sorrow and leads to joy.[49] The sorrow of repentance gives way to joy when we are forgiven and have the weight of guilt removed. The memory of evil brings joy when we see ourselves now free from it.[50] The repentant person sorrows about past pleasure that was wrong and rejoices at being restored to a good state of soul. Thus, not all sorrow is of present evil. As delight in evil is itself evil, so sorrow about evil is good. This sort of sorrow is good because it would be wrong not to feel sorrow about the evil one has committed. The greatest evil is not physical pain, as is often thought today, but guilt, because what harms the soul is worse than what harms the body.[51] Thus, not to think that evil is evil is a greater evil than any sorrow or pain, because this springs from a lack of judgment and right reason. To be deprived of these is an evil, because rationality constitutes the good of human nature.[52] Thus, repentance, like pity, is always a good sorrow.

As sorrow and joy are contrary emotions, so their manifestations have opposite effects. Laughing and smiling increase joy, but weeping does not increase sorrow; rather it lessens sorrow because to weep is visibly to let sorrow run out like water. To weep is to let out a harm that is shut up within one. The more a sorrow is locked up, the more the mind thinks about it; so to talk about it to a confidant lets it out and so lessens it. What expresses sorrow is weeping, which lessens it, but rejoicing increases joy.[53] The sad person is closed up in him or herself, but the joyful person goes out to others. Thus, it is natural to want to share one's joys with others—for example, a birthday or success in exams. In either way, one lets out joy or sorrow. When we share sorrow or grief with others, it is lessened because a burden is lightened when it is no longer carried alone but two carry it together. As Aristotle says, a sorrow shared is a sorrow halved.[54] But he does not add the opposite, which is equally true: a joy shared is a joy doubled, because one's own joy is increased by seeing other people rejoice at one's joy; their joy is added to one's own. We have a notable description of this in St. Thomas's commentary on the last article of the Apostles' Creed.

> (Eternal life), fourthly, consists in the joyful society of the blessed. This society will be especially delightful, because everyone will share every good thing with all the blessed. For everyone will love the other as himself, and so will rejoice in the good of another as his own. By this it comes about that the gladness and joy of one person is increased as much as the joy of all.

When people are joyful together, there is more joy; but when people are sorrowful together there is less sorrow.[55] The condolence of friends lessens the weight of sorrow as one sees oneself loved by them. The cause of this is that a friend's sorrow at one's own sorrow comes from his or her love, which we find pleasant.

Another way that sorrow is lessened is by contemplation of the truth, which brings the greatest of delights.[56] Since this is the highest joy, we can have this joy even in the midst of suffering when we raise our minds to divine things. Thus, in the midst of tribulation and discomfort, Boethius and St. Thomas More alike found comfort by turning their minds to things above this world. As they faced death during their imprisonment, Boethius wrote *The Consolation of Philosophy*, and St. Thomas More *A Dialogue of Comfort Against Tribulation*. The contemplation of truth softens sadness and pain, according to Aquinas, the more someone is a lover of wisdom (*amator sapientiae*).[57]

For sorrow, St. Thomas Aquinas prescribes four remedies: weeping, the company of friends, pleasure, and warm baths.[58]

(1) Weeping is a remedy, because it releases sorrow.

(2) The company of friends lightens the weight of sorrow. It is delightful to see oneself loved by friends. And when one sees that one is esteemed by friends, this increases the sense of one's own worth, which gives one encouragement. One cause of sorrow is to think that we are loved too little by others or less than we really are. Thus, an inferiority complex is a form of sorrow; it arises from having too poor an opinion of oneself. When we think that we are liked less by others than we really are, the sorrow is real but the motive illusory. Thus, the condolence of friends softens the sorrow.

(3) Pleasure is a remedy, because pleasure is to sorrow as rest is to physical tiredness. As rest is a remedy for the body, so pleasure is for the soul.[59]

(4) Warm baths are a remedy for sorrow, because sorrow distresses the body, so anything that restores the body to a good disposition also remedies sorrow. "Every good disposition of the body redounds to the heart."[60]

To sorrow with the sorrowing is the appropriate response to their state. As the appropriate response brings pleasure, so the inappropriate response causes pain. This pain is embarrassment. We experience embarrassment when our response is unexpectedly not accepted by another or we see someone else made to suffer pain before others. When someone laughs at the expense of another and sees this is painful for the other, we are caught between rejoicing with one and sorrowing with the other. When laughter and humor are inappropriate, they produce the opposite of their usual effect, because we are rejoicing when someone is in pain. Another source of embarrassment is when we do not treat another with the honor or seriousness they expect; we cause pain by misjudging their sensibility or dignity and are in turn pained by our own misjudgment.

A frequent form of sorrow today is depression, which used to be known by the name of "melancholy" until recent times. For example, when St. Teresa of Avila, in chapter seven of her *Book of the Foundations*, talks about melancholy, she is talking about what we call depression today. Another form of sorrow is disappointment, when we do not obtain or achieve the good result we hoped for. When this happens, hope turns into sorrow, not joy. We might think that resentment is also a form of sorrow, but it is closer to anger at wrong done to oneself. This seems to be where St. Thomas would place it. Interestingly, Latin has no special word for resentment: it is *ira* (anger). Resentment comes from not letting go of an injury of injustice and is thus a latent desire for revenge, which properly belongs to anger.

Anger

The spring of anger seems to be hate rather than love, but even here love is the cause of anger, because anger desires to avenge injustice. Thus, St. Thomas describes anger as the appetite for revenge. It arises from sadness at a wrong done to oneself. An angry person seeks the evil of harming someone under the aspect of the good of restoring justice.[61] It is natural for us to rise up against and resist what harms and does wrong to us. St. Thomas thought that there is something lacking in a person who is indifferent to injustice. Anger is good as long as it is controlled by reason and not directed against others out of proportion to the wrong done by them.

Anger turns to hate when it becomes hardened, but it differs from hate, as anger is directed against individuals but hate can be more general.[62] For example, people generally hate liars and thieves, the dishonest. Another difference is that anger passes more quickly than hate. As anger is a more transitory emotion, so its expression is more open. This explains why arguments that quickly flare up between motorists in the streets of Italy, for example, subside just as quickly. Hate tends to be more silent and is more lasting than anger. It agrees with anger in inflicting harm on another, but hate does it simply speaking, whereas anger intends it under the aspect of justice, of setting right a wrong.

Anger is the appetite to harm or attack another, but it wills evil to someone as the means of revenge. The motive of anger, St. Thomas says, is something done to oneself. We are also roused to anger at the harm done to others, but this is because we regard it as also done to ourselves.[63] It has a bad and a good aspect: to hurt another but in order to restore the good of justice. Anger may also move one to attack another when one is frustrated. It is bad when it is not tempered by reason. The evil of anger is that it prevents us from listening to the command of reason. Any passion prevents us from deliberating well, except that a little fear makes us more attentive as long as it does not affect reason.[64] Anger is unreasonable when the harm it intends to inflict is out of proportion to the wrong it seeks to address. The remedy for anger is gentleness, which softens it and makes us more receptive to others.

Anger is more natural than gentleness, because it is natural for animals to rise up with the irascible appetite against what opposes or hurts them.[65] To have virtue we require the balance of gentleness, since virtue is to act according to reason but anger impairs rational judgment. St. Thomas regarded gentleness as essential for virtue, since anger affects rational judgment. Gentleness, he says, makes a person master of him or herself (*compos*, which also suggests being composed).[66] A gentle answer breaks anger, because it is to lower oneself before the angry person, who ceases to be angry when he or she no longer has anything to attack. "A gentle answer breaks anger" (Prv 15:1). St. Thomas often quotes from the Book of Proverbs, which seems to have been of special interest to him.

Conversely, the lower the person who despises someone superior in social standing, authority, or ability, the greater the anger he or she thus provokes because the injury to the superior person is that much greater.[67] The lower despise those above them with less justice. The cause of anger in the superior person is sadness at the injury to his or her self-esteem.[68] Another form of contempt that provokes anger is the indifference of others to our interests, because when others despise what we think is important, we think ourselves to be despised.[69] Thus, sadness is a source of anger. We slight others when we regard what is important to them as of little importance. Anger arises when we meet with contempt, because we are frustrated at our own powerlessness and vulnerability.

Thus, St. Thomas names three causes of anger: it can arise from frustration, due to our vulnerability, or from contempt, or from indignation at injustice.[70]

Unlike the other emotions, which occur in pairs of contraries, anger has no contrary, because it contains in itself a mixture of contrary emotions.[71] It is caused by the contrary emotions of sadness and hope; sorrow at wrong done, and hope of revenge. As it has a double object, good and evil, so it is made up of contrary emotions: love of the good of justice, and hate of wanting to inflict the evil of harm.[72] A cause of anger is sadness, and an effect of it is delight, when revenge is obtained, for "vengeance is sweet."[73] Another reason why anger has no contrary is that there is no present good for this emotion to rest in; anger only attacks evil. There is no emotion of the irascible appetite for present good, because the irascible appetite only tends toward the good that is still future with hope, or it seeks to remove obstacles in the way of attaining this good with courage and anger.[74] Anger attacks what frustrates our desire or will. It has no contrary emotion, because it does not acquiesce in evil but only attacks it. The opposite of anger is ceasing from it. This is not an emotion but the absence of one. The only contrary of anger is gentleness, which is not an emotion but a virtue.

Thus, in St. Thomas, we naturally pass from the emotions to the virtues, which moderate and direct them. The usefulness of St. Thomas's psychology lies in its being founded on a complete view of human nature that integrates the sensitive and intellectual sides of it in a balanced life. He explains to us the natural mechanism of the emotions in everyday life as one releases or counteracts another. For St. Thomas, having good emotions is part of our perfection, because this requires the virtues. Virtue does not deprive us of our emotions but overcomes disordered emotions. There is a perfection in our lower, sensitive appetites when they obey reason easily. Reason governs or rules the appetites not as a despot rules over slaves but as a monarch rules over free subjects who can resist, St. Thomas says, quoting from Aristotle.[75] As the appetites can resist, so they can move the will. When the movements of our appetites share in reason, we establish an inner equilibrium in our person. The emotions need to be guided by reason; otherwise they conflict with one another. Thus, they are completed by the moral virtues. St. Thomas would have thought that we cannot establish order and balance in our affective lives without the virtues, and that the virtues provide the remedy for disorder of the emotions. Although some of the emotions share the same name as virtues—for example, love, hope, and courage—they differ, as the emotions are not dispositions for acting but rather reactions of the sensitive appetite to good and evil. The emotions are movements of the sensitive appetites, but the virtues enable us to act according to reason. St. Thomas notes that the emotions begin in the appetite and end in conformity with reason, but the virtues begin with reason and end in the appetite as it is moved by reason.[76] Thus, our next topic is the virtues.

8

The Virtues

St. Thomas seems to be the first person who wrote a work of what we call "moral theology." It is contained in the second part of the *Summa Theologiae* and takes up over half of the whole *Summa*. This second part is itself divided into two parts: the first part concerns general principles of moral action and concludes with the questions on law and grace. The second part treats the individual virtues with their opposite vices. This part is built on the four cardinal and three theological virtues. The cardinal virtues were inherited from the pagan Greek philosophers, as given to us in Plato. But they are also named together in scripture: "If anyone loves righteousness, her labors are virtues; for she teaches self-control and prudence, justice and courage" (Wis 8:7). St. Thomas defines virtue as an act consonant with reason.[1] "Since a human being is human, because he (or she) has reason, his good lies in being in accord with reason."[2] St. Thomas notes that there are three kinds of virtue: moral, intellectual, and theological. The moral virtues regulate the passions and only concern the appetites. Thus, we have justice for the rational appetite; the will; courage for the irascible appetite; and temperance for the desiring appetite. Here St. Thomas merely takes over the ethics of Aristotle, which are based on the structure of human nature. The intellectual virtues are for contemplating the truth; they include wisdom, understanding, and prudence.

The theological virtues are for reaching and uniting us with our last end, which is God. There are three theological virtues, St. Thomas says, because we need to know and desire the end in order to be moved to it in the right way. But the desire of the end requires two things: trust that the end can be obtained and love of the end. Thus, we know God by faith, we hope to attain him by hope, and love him by charity.[3] The moral and intellectual virtues are natural for all human beings, but we only have the theological virtues as we are sharers of grace.[4] By grace we are made sharers of divine nature, St. Thomas says, as wood shares in fire when it is set alight.[5]

St. Thomas notes that the cardinal virtues are so called because they are the hinges of the other virtues. One enters a house by the door. But we do not enter the house by the theological virtues; rather we go out by them to our last end. "The active life, which the moral virtues perfect, is the door to the contemplative life."[6] A virtue is a perfection of a power, St. Thomas says.[7] The virtues perfect us for actions that direct us to beatitude. Thus, Fergus Kerr, with good reason, suggests that we call the ethics of St. Thomas the ethics of beatitude rather than of virtue.[8] Although it is common to regard St. Thomas as presenting an ethics of virtue, because his ethics is based on Aristotle, he does not have an ethics of virtue in the proper sense, since contrary to Aristotle, he did not think that a good person produces good actions so much as good actions make a good person. For Aristotle good actions flow from the virtuous character, but for St. Thomas a person is good because he or she does good actions. We reach our end by our actions, and as Fergus Kerr notes, the end is important for Aquinas, whereas for Aristotle having good dispositions is primary.

There is a two-fold happiness: natural and supernatural. But Aquinas does not contrast a natural with a supernatural end, since he thinks that human nature has only one final end, even though it cannot be attained by our natural powers alone.[9] He rather contrasts imperfect with perfect beatitude. We can only have the former in this life, the latter only in the next life. The relation between the two has been nicely expressed by Ralph McInerny: St. Thomas does not distinguish two concepts of our end but two realizations of it: imperfect and perfect.[10]

The virtues do not perfect all our powers but those that are under the command of the will. As ethics is about human actions, and actions are specifically human because they are voluntary, we should first look at St. Thomas's theory of the will before going on to his teaching about virtues.

The Will

The will is the appetite of reason. An appetite is an inclination to something good (we are not inclined to evil but run away from it). We will ends, but only reason apprehends an end as an end. Animals also apprehend ends but not as ends. We can select vastly more ends than other animals, because we are not limited to the appetites of sense but also have reason. The relation between reason and will in St. Thomas is that reason directs us to an end and the will moves us to where reason directs it.[11] Thus, reason gives us a compass bearing, so to speak, and when I have got my bearing, the will moves me in that direction. St. Thomas also compares the two by saying that reason gives the order and the will executes what reason apprehends, just as a general gives the command that others then execute. Thus, reason is the strongest of our powers, St. Thomas says, because it commands the others.

A voluntary act has two essential features: it has an intrinsic principle, or source, of action, and it comes from one's own inclination. It is also done with knowledge. Animals have an intrinsic source of action, but they do not act for ends, because you have to know an end to do this. They are moved to their ends by natural instinct, as when birds build nests for rearing their young. Animals only have the basic ends of living and reproducing, but we have vastly more varied and higher ends because we have reason, which can apprehend more ends than the basic ones of nature. Animals and birds move toward something to which their natural appetite is inclined as soon as it is presented to them. They follow the impulses of passion, because they have no reason in them. They do not choose between ends, because they cannot order them with reason.[12] Will, in the proper sense, only exists where it is possible to choose between alternative courses of action. Animals have some kind of choice but not will, because only deliberation envisages opposite courses of action, and only reason deliberates. Animals do not deliberate about their acts, because they lack reason and so will. It is because we can deliberate about our actions that we have dominion over them and are master of ourselves. It is having dominion over our actions that makes us truly free.

According to Aquinas, an action can still be voluntary even when it is not directly willed. As he observes, not to will is also a voluntary choice.[13] A captain is responsible for letting his ship run aground even when he did not intend to, if this occurs through his not willing to steer the ship at the time. One can either will not to act or simply fail to will: in both cases, the result is voluntary because one can err by not willing. For example, "I do not wish to speak" may mean either I will not to speak or I simply do not will at all. Omission and negligence are also voluntary.

An action is voluntary because the inclination proceeds from within. It is contrary to the idea of voluntary action that it can be compelled or forced. Force and coercion come from outside. Although God moves the will every time that we act virtuously, God does not compel the will, although he is more powerful, because he moves the will according to its nature. St. Thomas quotes Proverbs 21:1: "The heart of the king is in the hand of God, who inclines it in whatever direction he wills."[14] We could not will anything unless God first moved the will to its universal object, which is the good. As St. Thomas says, no one can will anything without being moved by the Mover of all things to the good.[15] Only reason apprehends universals like existence, the good, and the true. Animals only want particular good things, because they are limited to the senses. A cat wants this mouse but not health in general. But unlike animals, human beings are not necessarily moved by appetite because, although we cannot prevent desire from arising, we can will not to consent. The will moves voluntarily, although it is moved by God, because it is sufficient that the source of action lies within the agent, but the first principle does not have to be intrinsic in the series of those who move and are moved.[16]

St. Thomas considers the objection that when God moves the will, the will is necessarily moved and cannot resist him— otherwise God would be ineffective. In reply, he quotes Ecclesiasticus 4:18, "God constituted man from the beginning and left him in the hand of his counsel." If God moved the will by necessity, it would not be a will that he moved. An act is still voluntary although the will is moved by another, when the extrinsic principle is the cause of all nature and will. God does not move the will against its nature. He is the cause of will as he is of the rational soul that is created by him. An angel cannot move the will directly from within but only tempt someone by presenting outside objects that are attractive.

Sometimes actions done out of fear seem to be involuntary, for instance, when Christians were commanded to sacrifice to idols. Here St. Thomas says that, although we do not will the act itself, it is voluntary because we desire to avoid the evil that we fear, namely of losing one's life. Thus, Christians seemingly compelled to sacrifice to idols acted voluntarily in that they desired to retain their life. Likewise, a captain does not will to jettison his cargo, but he does so voluntarily in order to save his ship from sinking. Here he wills the end of saving his ship, although he does not want the means. Thus, an act done out of fear is voluntary, because something (to save life) is willed. St. Thomas also asks whether the intemperate act involuntarily when they are overcome by desire. Here the cause is not quite the same as with fear, because what we fear is contrary to our will but what is pleasant is consonant with the will, as the appetite is naturally inclined to what is good in itself. Thus, things done through passion are more voluntary than those done out of fear, in St. Thomas's opinion.[17] Although desire can take away reason, what is done unknowingly is still voluntary, because one freely chooses the action that takes away reason, for instance, when someone having taken drugs has no control and runs another down in the street. Ignorance only excuses when due precaution has been taken and you regret what has been done. In all these cases, St. Thomas's principle is that an action is only involuntary when it is against one's own will, and it is only against one's will when it causes something that displeases you.[18]

In willing the end, one also wills the means, although one may not want the means. One wills the end and the other things as they are directed to the end. For example, if I will health and to be cured, I will the treatment however disagreeable it may be. We will the end, for example health, and *deliberate* about the means: whether to consult a doctor, take herbal medicines, or visit spa waters. We will the means by willing the end.[19] We naturally will some things, St. Thomas says: to exist and live and to know the truth and the ultimate end of the will, which is the good. As the will moves us from what is possible to an actual state, he says that it comes between reason and action.[20]

St. Thomas observes that the will is both moved and moves. As it is not always actually willing, but sometimes wills and sometimes is inactive, it needs to be moved by something. St. Thomas says that it is moved by appetite and by reason. But the reason's apprehension of the true only moves the will under the idea of the good.[21] We are first moved by the end, which is something perceived as good. The end is presented to the will by reason. In this way the will is moved by the intellect. The will moves itself by willing the end presented to it by reason. The will is also moved by the appetites but is not forced, because this is according to the inclination of its own nature.[22] The will is not moved by necessity because it can envisage opposites; it is open to alternative courses of action and can move either way. The intellect necessarily assents to self-evident principles, such as nothing can both exist and not exist at the same time, but the will does not necessarily consent to its object. The will would only be necessarily inclined to the object proposed to it if this were good in every respect; it can only not want the perfect good, which is beatitude. But as all particular good things in this life fall short of the perfect good, the will does not necessarily choose any of them.[23] Only the final end is not in our choice, because no one chooses not to be happy.[24]

Contrary to belief in astrology, which is as popular today as it was in the Middle Ages, St. Thomas says that the heavenly bodies only *seem* to move the will, because many people follow the passions of their bodily constitution ("complexion" is St. Thomas's word). Thus, the heavenly bodies affect people's temperaments and lives because they affect their bodies and so the emotions of their sense appetites.[25] But the heavenly bodies cannot directly move the will itself, because it is an immaterial power, as it goes with the intellect.

Prudence

St. Thomas says that a human being is human because he or she has reason, and we attain reason in acting by the virtue of prudence. Prudence is the virtue for perfecting our reason, as the moral virtues perfect the appetites: justice the will (rational appetite), fortitude the irascible appetite, and temperance the desiring appetite.[26] The moral virtues preserve the good of reason in the face of sudden impulse and passion. Although prudence is often counted as one of the moral virtues, properly speaking prudence is one of the intellectual virtues. It perfects *practical* reason, whereas wisdom and understanding perfect the speculative intellect. Virtue needs to be perfected by reason because it is not in us by nature, except as an aptitude for the good. Perfect virtue is not in us by nature, because reason is open to many possibilities. Many people today have a wrong idea of prudence: they associate it with being cautious, taking care that one does not suffer loss, insuring oneself against loss, and being on the safe side. For St. Thomas, it is a positive virtue that knows how to apply the right principle in every situation. Contrary to modern concepts of moral virtue, virtue for St. Thomas is not primarily about obeying rules. It is just the virtue of prudence that frees us from having to refer to the book of rules to see what is right in any situation, and gives us a confident command of applying principles rightly in new situations on our own. Prudence establishes right reason about things to be *done*, whereas the virtues of the speculative intellect are for the truth that is to be *known*.

As prudence perfects reason for things to be done, it concerns individual, contingent matters; St. Thomas says that it applies universal principles to particular situations, which are variable and uncertain. It requires two things: knowledge of general principles and experience.[27] It is not primarily about being aware of snares, although it includes taking care and having foresight; it is rather about the right end. A good thief also takes precautions, but he is not prudent; rather he has cunning or astuteness. To have a virtue, the end needs to be good. A thief has false prudence. Caution is a part of prudence, so that we are injured less by the attacks of fortune, because evil is mixed with the good in this life. But prudence finds the right means to the end. Reason first apprehends the possible courses of action; then counsel (*eubulia*) deliberates. The choice of one of the alternatives is made by the judgment, and the will commands the choice to be put into action.[28] Thus, in every action there are three stages: deliberation, judgment, and the command of the will. The choice itself, Aquinas says, follows the judgment of reason. A person has the virtue of prudence when he or she deliberates well about the means ordered to the end. There is no prudence without deliberating well, but prudence is also perceptive: it not only deliberates but also *commands*, because it is about putting one's choice *into action*.[29] The principal act of prudence, St. Thomas says, is to command. We command not only others but ourselves too when reason commands the lower appetites. *Eubulia* only takes counsel. The other technical Greek term that St. Thomas uses in his account of prudence is *synesis*— this means judgment. One who chooses well the means to the end in practical affairs has true but imperfect prudence, St. Thomas says, not perfect prudence, which concerns the end of one's *whole* life.[30]

The principle part of prudence, for St. Thomas, is providence, because it is about ordering things, just as God by his providence orders the whole universe. Indeed St. Thomas sees a close connection between the Latin words *prudentia* and *providentia*. Prudence includes being provident about the future—for example, laying up some of the harvest for a time of need.[31] We should have solicitude about the needs of others rather than our own. But it is only sinful to have solicitude about the future if we make temporal concerns our end or seek superfluous things beyond what is necessary for this life. The rule, St. Thomas says, is that "our solicitude should principally be about spiritual goods, hoping that the temporal will also fall to us in what we need, if we do what is our duty."[32] He remarks that Christians know more about divine providence than pagans did, so they do not need to take so much solicitude for themselves.

St. Thomas says that choice is of the means, intention of the end you intend to achieve by the means.[33] The intention does not by itself make the will good: one may have a good intention but a bad will, for instance, to steal in order to give alms to the poor.[34] A bad intention makes the will bad, but a good will is not enough by itself. Prudence is also needed for acting in the right way. Prudence especially demands the mean in acting, for we can err by falling short of or exceeding reason. For example, we can be too timid or too bold. The mean between the two, of being neither too fearful nor too daring, is the virtue of fortitude, which restrains fear and audacity alike; Shakespeare seems to have had in mind this teaching of Aristotle's that virtue lies in the mean between the two extremes of too little and too much, when he makes Nerissa say: "It is no mean happiness to be seated in the mean."[35] Shakespeare assumes Aristotle's view that the end of virtue is happiness. Virtue lies in the mean, because emotion can fall short of or exceed the rule of reason by, for instance, having too much or too little of desire or audacity.

In order to be prudent we also need to be docile, as St. Thomas says. Docility, from the Latin *docibilis*, does not mean soft and yielding, as is often thought today, but the ability to be taught, literally teachableness. We need this for prudence, in St.

Thomas's view, because it concerns what is to be done, but no one can consider all that is to be done, because the possibilities are infinite in diversity; so a person needs to be instructed about them.[36] Prudence is required as it applies universal principles to particular situations, but whoever errs about the principles will also go wrong about the other virtues, for prudence is right reason about the principles of action. Prudence judges correctly about what is to be done on this particular occasion, in these circumstances.[37] Prudence considers human affairs; wisdom the highest cause of all, God. Perfect prudence takes counsel about what is the good end of the whole of life. Thus, prudence considers the means that bring us to felicity, and wisdom considers the object of felicity that makes us happy. Using the same analogy as he does for the relation of the cardinal to the theological virtues, St. Thomas likens prudence to the doorkeeper who introduces us to the king, who is wisdom.[38]

But prudence is not perfect without charity, because charity directs us to our final end.[39] As St. Thomas says, a person attains right reason through prudence, but God through charity. Prudence unites the natural virtues, as charity unites the supernatural virtues. We need prudence, because virtues can be imperfect or perfect. We can have some of them imperfectly without having others, but we cannot have them perfectly without having all the virtues. The perfect virtues are all connected. As already stated one needs prudence because the virtues are not perfect without it. St. Thomas quotes St. Gregory the Great: "Unless one acts prudently, they are not true virtues."[40]

The Unity of the Virtues

St. Thomas clearly upheld the thesis of the unity of the virtues: that one cannot have the virtues without having them all, for one cannot have prudence without the moral virtues, and one cannot have the moral virtues properly without prudence. As we shall see, each of the cardinal virtues has something of the individual character of each of the other three. The cardinal virtues are united, because there is one virtue that directs them: prudence. The virtues are also united, because the emotions are united, as they all spring from love or hate and end in sorrow or joy.[41] The virtues are united, because the choice of the end depends on being well disposed; and this in turn depends on the uprightness (rectitude) of our appetites. "Prudence requires a correct disposition in our emotions and affections."[42] Conversely, the moral virtues require prudence, because choice comes from reason, which is perfected by prudence. Prudence requires the moral virtues, because the passions can blind the judgment of reason. Prudence also requires the moral virtues, because "as a person is, so does the end appear to him."[43]

What is special to each cardinal virtue should be common to them all, St. Thomas says.[44] Prudence possesses the idea of discretion. Discretion has much the same role as prudence in the Rule of St. Benedict, which has considerably shaped the culture of western Europe. Firmness in fortitude needs to be exercised with discretion, lest we are too inflexible. Temperance requires discretion lest I become too ascetical or strict when charity requires otherwise. Justice has the idea of rightness. Prudence is the good of reason in commanding, and justice the good of reason in activity. Fortitude has the idea of firmness for standing firm in the good of reason against the impulse of passion. The temperate person needs firmness in forgoing pleasures. Conversely the brave person has temperance, because he or she is not broken by the attraction of pleasure. St. Thomas notes that it is little use having strength of mind through fortitude but without discretion, rectitude of will, and moderation, which is of the essence of temperance.[45] As he says, temperance requires fortitude and is also likely to be just, in that the intemperate person is likely to take more than his or her fair share. Temperance should be firm and fortitude tempered. Likewise, one needs to be firm to maintain justice in all one's business transactions, rather than compromise one's principles for the sake of quick gain; but one also needs to temper justice lest one be too strict or legalistic.

There is a unity of the virtues, because what makes someone good is a good will, and we use all our other powers of the soul by the will. But what makes the will good is the moral virtues.[46] Jean Porter has observed that inner unity is essential to having peace.[47]

Justice

St. Thomas describes justice thus: "Justice concerns the good of equality in things pertaining to the common life."[48] Here we may note the two main characteristics of justice: it is a kind of equality, and it is directed to the common good. Prudence is concerned with the good of the human being, but justice with the good of others. Thus, St. Thomas regards justice as the greatest of the moral virtues: it is greater than the others as the common good is greater than the good of the individual.[49] As justice is concerned with the common good and involves equality, but nothing is equal to itself, justice clearly concerns things that belong to another.[50] Justice establishes equality in things belonging to another.

There are two kinds of justice, as it establishes rightness in exchange and distribution. Distributive justice, which is often overlooked today, is concerned with the distribution of common goods to individuals according to their honor or position in society. It sees to the distribution of the goods of the community to individual persons as they are parts of a whole.[51] Thus, the head of state or monarch receives a larger dwelling and household because of his or her position, and he or she is supported by the people by distributive justice. When people call for the abolition of the monarchy because of the extra cost to the state, they overlook the notion of distributive justice. It is just that individuals who have special responsibility for, and duties to, the community or society receive more than an equal share.

Commutative justice, on the other hand, is characterized by strict equality. Everyone is, or should be, equal when it comes to paying the price for some goods: a prince has to pay for a pair of shoes the same as a pauper. Distributive justice preserves the correct proportion between people; commutative justice equality. It is unjust to take away from others what belongs to them. There are three areas in which commutative justice especially applies: possessions, persons, and work. To take away from a person's honor or reputation by detraction, slander, or false accusation is unjust as to take their possessions is theft. We can harm others by bodily injury or injury to their reputation. Thus, damages are awarded to compensate for loss of health or of good name when someone is injured in either of these two ways. It is only right that labor should be repaid with an equal wage for expenditure of energy; one should reward those from whose labor one benefits.

St. Thomas provides some useful guidelines for justice in buying and selling.[52] An article may be sold for more than it is worth either because of some mistake about its nature, its quantity, or its quality. For instance, a bag may be sold as real leather when it is an imitation, a painting as a genuine Turner when it is a fake; or the scales may be false and the fishmonger may hand over fish that weighs less than what you pay for; or an article may be sold with some defect, so that it does not work. In all these cases if the seller is unaware of the mistake, he or she does not sell unjustly but is bound to make restitution when the fault comes to light. On the other hand, the buyer may get something for much less than it is really worth. The buyer buys unjustly if he or she knows that the article is under-priced, for the buyer exploits the ignorance of the seller. In this case the buyer must compensate the seller. For example, one may discover that one has two pieces of paper on returning home when the assistant in the shop thought she was wrapping one and so only charged for one. Goods, however, may be sold for more than their value when the seller is parting with something that is dear to him or her and the buyer greatly wants or needs it. In times of famine the price of corn may be increased due to demand; this is to regulate the distribution, so that no one buys too much and everyone can buy some. But the price should not be raised so much that the seller exploits the needy. St. Thomas says that the manufacturers may sell their wares at a profit in order to earn a living but not for the love of inordinate gain. The profit one makes should be honest, either to help one's family or the poor.

St. Thomas also provides some other interesting side-lights on justice. For example, he considers the question whether a judge is unjust if he, say, acquits a person on the evidence presented in court when he knows this person to be guilty because of something he knows privately. In this case, St. Thomas says that the judge is just, although he knows his judgment is contrary to the truth, because a judge is the interpreter of the law, and so must judge according to the laws and what is proved in court. He does not have to bring in what is only known to him privately.[53] St. Thomas reminds us that a judge judges between others, not himself and others.

For St. Thomas, a part of justice is the virtue of truth. Truth is a part of justice, because "one person owes it to another out of honesty to make known the truth."[54] Since we are by nature social beings, we owe to one another that on which society depends, and one of these things is trust. It is not possible to trust untruthful people. Veracity or truthfulness is a part of the virtue of justice in two respects, as justice involves equality and concerns others. To speak the truth is an equality between saying things greater than what is true about oneself by boasting and exaggerating and what is less than the truth by understatement or irony.[55] Truth is also a mean between saying superfluous things when it is inopportune and saying less than one ought by hiding what should be made known. As Aquinas says, the virtue of truth lies in an equality of the mind or of the signs (words) with what we think of or signify, just as truth itself, in St. Thomas's definition, is a correspondence or matching (*adaequatio*) of the mind with reality. We can fail in this virtue by saying too much or too little, but the latter is less against the virtue. St. Thomas allows that one may say less than one ought by denying something out of prudence, which he says should be preserved in all the virtues.[56] There is a special virtue for truth but not for the good, he says, because truth is a special good but the good belongs to the whole class of the virtues.

Justice is like charity in that they are both virtues of the will, but they also differ in two respects. Justice seeks the good of others, but charity raises the will to the divine good.[57] Justice concerns the good of the other, but charity loves the other. As justice preserves the common good, it directs us to a good that transcends the individual.[58] As Jean Porter again says, justice directs the good of the individual to the common good that protects the good of the individual. The attainment of our individual good depends on our relation to society, and as she points out, a good relation to society presupposes order and integrity in our own life. Here again we see the unity of the virtues, as each one requires the others. For order in our selves we have the affective virtues of fortitude and temperance, which restrain the fear of pain and desire of pleasure when these may tempt to act contrary to our good. Justice differs from the affective virtues, because it regulates exterior actions but the affective virtues control inner passions. Justice concerns activities; the affective virtues concern passions and emotions.

Fortitude and Temperance

Fortitude, or courage, is firmness of spirit in doing good and bearing evils. It stands firm in resisting evils.[59] It is the virtue for when we meet with adversity. Fortitude is accompanied by patience, which St. Thomas describes as an ornament of fortitude. Patience preserves the good of reason in the face of sorrow and pain. It makes us reasonable, so that we see our own sorrows in perspective and are not overwhelmed by them. Thus, patience helps us to keep a just estimate of reality. Patience sustains evils for the sake of some good—for example, hardship for the sake of saving money to pay for children's education. It also keeps out the sorrow that is the root of anger, resentment, hate, and vengeance. Patience differs from fortitude as it concerns sorrows, but fortitude concerns dangers. Patience bears present suffering; fortitude corrects fears, which are of future evils. Fortitude sustains actions when we might withdraw from our good purpose because of difficulty and danger.

Temperance prevents us from turning from the good of reason through the influence of passion. Temperance restrains passion, especially the pleasure of touch, St. Thomas says.[60] It
checks the desires that obscure reason.

Infused Virtue

As St. Thomas says that the cardinal virtues are for steering
our ship through this life,[61] we may extend his analogy and add
that the end of steering a ship is to bring it safely into port. To
reach the harbor of eternal life, the virtues that we require by our
own acts are not enough; we also need virtue that is infused by
God as a divine gift. The acquired virtues are not enough,
because we are also made to be citizens of a heavenly city: "you
are citizens with all the saints" (Eph 2:19). The infused virtues
make us participants of the heavenly city.[62] As St. Thomas
explains the difference: acquired virtues direct us to being citizens on earth; the infused virtues to the glory of celestial life.
The difference between acquired and infused virtue is as it
orders us to this life or eternal life.[63] Temperance, for example,
can be an acquired or infused virtue. As an acquired virtue it
seeks the mean in pleasure that is directed to our good in this
life. As an infused virtue it directs us to eternal life. It is the difference between being temperate for the sake of health, or any
reason purely for this life, and forgoing pleasure for the sake of
doing penance and offering a sacrifice to atone for others as
well. As St. Thomas notes, it is not required that one be a good
sailor or business person to have the infused virtue of prudence,
which looks to one's salvation. The acquired virtues relate us to
others; the infused to God.[64]

There is a good that is proportioned, or measured, to our
nature and there is a good that surpasses it. To be fitted for attaining this latter good, our nature by itself is not enough; it needs to
be raised up by grace. Because our end is a supernatural one, we
need perfections of our powers, which exceed the capacity of our
nature. Thus, we also need the infused virtues, which direct us to
our final end. All the infused virtues are given with charity, which
fulfills the Law.[65] As we shall see in the next chapter, the Law

itself presupposes the moral virtues, and these are infused with charity which fulfils the law. This means that the possession of the supernatural virtue of charity makes our natural virtues into infused ones, for they are now exercised with a new motive and governing principle.

Charity is the end of the Law, because all the precepts of the Law involve the virtues, and the virtues are directed to the theological virtues of faith, hope, and charity as their end. Faith shows us the end, hope enables us to tend toward it, and charity unites us with it. The moral virtues dispose us to our end by correcting the passion of the desiring appetite with temperance, the emotions of the irascible appetite (fear and audacity) with fortitude, and anger with gentleness. Justice corrects us in relation to our neighbor, and prudence disposes us for having faith, as it is the virtue for reason. Faith is directed toward charity because, in St. Thomas's view, you need faith to have charity.

> Those who do not have true faith cannot love God, because whoever believes falsely does not yet love God. A person who does not believe does not love, because affection is not fixed except in what the intellect shows it.[66]

No single virtue can be perfect without charity, and with charity all the other virtues are given. "Whoever has charity must have all the other virtues. But charity is in a person by being infused by God."[67] Thus, all the virtues, cardinal and theological, are directed to charity.

Although we shall no longer exercise certain virtues that we need in this life because of our corporeal nature, like temperance, fortitude, and justice, they will remain in the next life, St. Thomas says, just as a man who stands bravely in battle is still brave when he rejoices in victory afterward.[68] Justice and prudence remain, because the will and reason remain subject to God in heaven. He quotes Wisdom 1:5, "Justice is immortal." Fortitude and temperance remain after the resurrection, because the appetites of the body will be subject to reason in the blessed.[69] As St. Augustine said that a person is his or her choices (*voluntates*), so perhaps

St. Thomas would have said that a human being is his or her virtues, for it is the cardinal virtues that make us truly human, and faith, hope, and charity that direct us to our final end.

9

The Old Law

The Old Law may not appear to be a particularly attractive topic today, but anyone who reads St. Thomas will soon notice that it frequently comes into his works. Indeed it is indispensable for understanding what he has to say about Redemption by Christ. This should hardly surprise us, as it is not possible to understand the New Testament apart from the Old Testament, which prepared the way for the former. St. Thomas's views on the Old Law have an added interest as they also tell us about his attitude to the Jews when there has been renewed interest among historians in the relations of Christians and Jews in the Middle Ages. Jewish scholars were, with Arabs, part of the intellectual world that eventually brought Aristotle's works to western Europe a century before St. Thomas's lifetime. We have already noted, in chapter one, St. Thomas's acquaintance with, and debt to, the Jewish thinker Maimonides. But some historians when discussing Aquinas's attitude to the Jews make no mention of what he has to say about the Old Law, which is surely where we find his true thought on the question.

St. Thomas held quite enlightened views about Jews in an age when their persecution by Christians could still break out. For example, on the question of whether Jewish children should be baptized as Christians against the will of their parents, St. Thomas took the line that this practice was to be discouraged on grounds of natural justice, because children belong by nature to their parents.[1] He also held that the rites of the Jews should be tolerated and the Jews be allowed to observe their feasts, although the Old Law had now been superseded by the Christian religion, because their rites at least witness to the Christian faith and are a figure of what Christians believe.[2]

The first thing to be said about the Old Law is that it is *divine*: that is, it has been promulgated by God. St. Thomas distinguishes the Old from the New Law as the imperfect from the perfect. Thus, the Old Law was not given by God made man, like the perfect law, but either through Moses and Aaron, or through angels, as St. Paul says in Galatians 3:19.[3] It was also given to only one race, Israel, although the salvation it promised was meant for all nations, because God's promise to the Patriarchs was that Christ would spring from them.[4] Thus, this race was not chosen for any merit of its own but by grace, which is God's love (*dilectio*). God made this single race holy for himself, because this Mediator between God and the human race was to come from it. God chose one race, because Christ could only be descended from one race in his human nature. The Old and the New Law have a similar end, because there is one God who is the author of both Testaments; but they differ by being further from, and nearer to, their end. Although they have the same end, they also differ as imperfect and perfect.

Law exists to maintain the common good of society and the order of justice and virtue. The end of human law is the tranquility of the state, but this does not suffice for the end of divine law, which is to lead us to eternal felicity. This end, however, was blocked by sin. Thus, the Old Law was unable to bring human beings to their end, because only the grace of the Holy Spirit can make us suited to it; but to give this grace was reserved to Christ alone, as the Holy Spirit proceeds from the Father and the Son.

The role of the Old Law was to direct men and women to Christ. It did this in two ways. First, it witnessed to Christ. Second, it disposed them for salvation, first by drawing them away from idolatry, which is the worship of false gods, and second by gathering them in worship of the one true God, by whom the human race is saved through Jesus Christ. It is for this reason that the Old Law contains not only moral precepts but also many prescriptions for the correct worship of God. These are the ceremonial precepts. The Old Law also includes ceremonial precepts because law exists to order human beings not only one to another but also to God.

Natural Law

Many of the moral precepts of the Old Law are the same as the natural law, which is the moral law that can be known by natural reason alone. Indeed St. Thomas says that all the moral precepts of the Old Law come under the natural law.[5] St. Thomas introduces the concept of natural law as a part of providence, which we saw in chapter three to be God's plan for guiding the universe. Law is the plan in the ruler's mind for what is to be done by those subject to him; it is "the law of the dictate of practical reason governing a community."[6] In St. Thomas's view, the whole universe is governed by law, since everything comes under providence. Thus, the universe is ruled by *eternal* law.

Natural law is but "a participation by rational creatures in the eternal law."[7] This means that natural law is part of divine providence. We have this participation in the eternal law through the use of human reason, because the light of natural reason is itself an imprint of the divine light in us. St. Thomas thought that we can either know things in themselves or by their effects, in which a likeness of them is found, as when we know the sun by seeing the rays of light that it throws out. Only the blessed know the eternal law in the first way, "but every rational creature is able to know it more or less by the light that shines from it," for all knowledge of the truth is, St. Thomas says, a kind of "irradiation".[8] There has recently been a certain amount of dispute about whether natural law can be known by itself apart from some knowledge of God. As it is, in St. Thomas's definition, a participation in the eternal law, does it not presuppose belief in God? Anthony Lisska argues that the concept of natural law can stand by itself; Russell Hittenger that it cannot, because the very idea of it comes from Christian theology. Fergus Kerr makes the valid point that we cannot dissociate natural law from God, because every law depends on a lawgiver.[9] It should, however, be remembered that the idea of natural law goes back to the Stoics; for example, Panaetius (ca. 180–109 BC) saw in nature a standard of morality.

St. Thomas thought that the general principles of natural law can be known by everyone, since people recognize that things for which everyone has a natural inclination are good and, therefore, what is detrimental to them is bad. St. Thomas says that those things belong to natural law to which we are inclined by nature. Natural reason apprehends certain things to be good for human beings, because we have a natural inclination for them. He divides these things into three groups. First is what we share with all substances, which is to preserve our own existence. This includes the protection of life. Then follow the traits we share with other animals, such as reproduction of species. Thus, it is good for husband and wife to be joined together, and children to be educated. Third is what is specific to human beings, which is reason. Thus, it is good for human beings to know the truth, including the truth about God, and to live in society, for we depend on others to learn the truth. From this we can see that ignorance is to be avoided and we should not offend others. The first principle of natural law, St. Thomas says, is: "Good is to be done and evil to be avoided." All the other precepts of natural law are founded on this one.[10]

Some people argue against the idea that there is a law that can be known by everyone by natural reason, because not everyone can agree on the basic human goods that it is always wrong to destroy. St. Thomas, however, in answer to the question of whether there is one law of nature for everyone, replies that its first principles are the same for everyone, although people differ about the conclusions they draw from these principles, but this difference is due to reason having been depraved either by passion or evil custom. In support of his view he quotes a pagan, Julius Caesar, who said that robbery is against the law of nature.[11]

The place of law in St. Thomas's ethics has come to be revalued. Maria Carl points out that writers on St. Thomas used to concentrate on his theory of natural law but now this is thought to make his moral theology seem to be legalistic, whereas scholars now recognize that it is founded on the virtues. But some writers now go to the opposite extreme in omitting natural law as of any importance in St. Thomas's thought. Maria Carl's view is that the two approaches are not exclusive but go together, for the end of the law is to command actions that lead us to happiness.[12] As we noted in the previous chapter, St. Thomas says that virtues perfect us for actions that lead to beatitude. Carl points out that to depreciate the role of law in St. Thomas's thought is to undermine his theory of the virtues, because the law commands acts, and the virtues dispose us for performing these acts.[13] Natural law prescribes acts of virtue, and natural law includes things for which we have a natural inclination, among which is to act according to reason, the very definition of virtue. Thus, Maria Carl sees law and virtue as complementary in the moral theology of St. Thomas. His ethics is based on natural inclinations, and natural law is what we can know about acting in accordance with these inclinations by reason.

We are directed to our proper end by law, but as our last end lies beyond nature, we need divine law as well as natural law. Thus, the Old Law was made known by God in addition to the natural law that can be known by natural reason. Natural law and the Old Law are not two different or separate laws, but the same law known in two different ways by the same light of reason and by a divine promulgation. The divine law even presupposes natural law, St. Thomas says, just as grace presupposes nature, on which it builds.[14] But it also adds to natural law precepts about the worship of God. St. Thomas thought that it was part of justice that we obey God as something we owe to him, because we are by nature subject to him.

Divine Law

As all the moral precepts of the Old Law can be known by natural reason, why was it necessary for God to promulgate the Old Law? St. Thomas answers that the Old Law was given for a time, to let human beings recognize their need for the grace of Christ on seeing that they were unable to observe it by their own strength, so that they would have recourse to the help of grace.[15] But, unlike the Reformers in the sixteenth century, St. Thomas did not think that this was the sole or main purpose of the Old Law—to make us aware of how far we fall short of command- ments of God by our own powers. The Old Law was given for three reasons. First, so that men would not think that human reason by itself was sufficient for salvation. Second, to remedy our ignorance about the moral law. And third, so that men would not be proud of their own strength and knowledge. In his *Commentary on the Letter to the Galatians*, Aquinas gives another set of three reasons why the law was given by God: to withdraw men who were badly disposed from sin, and to make clear to us the weakness of our knowledge and strength, so that, recogniz- ing their infirmity and imperfection, human beings would seek the grace of the Mediator.[16] He adds that, although the natural law can be known by everyone, we also need the moral law to be made known by God because human reason has been darkened by sin and so is liable to err about what is good and evil.

The intention of natural law, St. Thomas says, is friendship between human beings, and of the divine law, friendship with God as well as with one another.[17] Indeed St. Thomas thought that if friendship prevailed among every society, there would be no need for laws about justice; men would behave justly to one another and themselves. Thus, friendship rather than justice is the basis of society for him, as it was for Aristotle too, since it is friendship that brings people together in the first place. St. Thomas explains that the Old Law contains moral precepts because only good men can truly be friends and they cannot be good without having the virtues. The law tends to constitute friendship, because the end of the law, St. Thomas reminds us, is charity.[18] As we shall see in the final chapter, charity is a part of friendship for St. Thomas. As the purpose of the law is friendship with other human beings and God, so the whole law is summed up in the double commandment of charity: to love God, and one's neighbor, as oneself. But we only really love ourselves in directing ourselves to God, for this is our good as it is our proper end. The great Commandment is itself a combination of two commandments of the Old Law: Deuteronomy 6:5 and Leviticus 19:18. Although the great Commandment to love God and neighbor is not one of the Ten Commandments, St. Thomas says that it is contained in them as a principle is contained in the conclusions derived from it.[19] The Old Law virtually gives the command of charity, but not the Holy Spirit, by whom charity is poured out into our hearts. Indeed we cannot keep the commandments without also having charity, because they presuppose it. Thus, the essence of the Decalogue for St. Thomas is not so much a set of prohibitions as friendship with God, although it also contains prohibitions because these tell us what destroys friendship with God.

The Old and New Law

It is common to describe the difference between the Old and New Law as that between fear and love. The Old Law is supposed to have induced men to obey it out of fear of punishment, as the New Law does so out of love. The Old Law restrains by fear of punishment, the New inclines use by the promise of eternal things. St. Thomas remarks that there is an element of fear in all law, because precepts of the law have the power to coerce. Even charity is commanded by the law because, although love of its nature can only be spontaneously given, charity directs our actions to God. St. Thomas says, however, that we do not have to keep the commandments out of love as long as we do keep them. But charity belongs to keeping them perfectly, and thus it is the fulfillment of the law.

Since the Old Law was instituted to order society, and, therefore, to order human beings to God, it included ceremonial laws for the acts of religion. The worship of God is exterior and interior, just as we consist of body and soul. Exterior acts of worship lead to the union of mind and heart with God. External religion consists of rites and ceremonies, such as we find in the Old Law. External worship is directed to internal worship, as the worship of the New Law is "in spirit and truth" (Jn 4:23). Internal religion consists in faith, hope, and charity.[20] St. Thomas considered that "there are some in the state of the Old Law, having charity and the grace of the Holy Spirit, who belonged in this respect to the New Law. . . . But even though the Old Law gave the precepts of charity, it did not give the Holy Spirit, by which charity is poured into our hearts."[21]

The external worship of the Old Law is, first, of a figure of Christ and, second, of the truth that will only be manifest in our heavenly homeland (*in patria*). The way that leads to the truth in our heavenly home is Christ. This way is revealed to us in the New Law. The Old Law is related to the New as a shadow to the image, and the New Law is related to the end of our home in heaven as an image to the truth.[22] Thus, St. Thomas sees everything as directed to the end of glory in heaven. The role of the two laws may thus be represented by the following diagram.

Old Law	New Law	In Patria
prefigures	Christ, the way to	glory
shadow	image	truth

The sacrifices of the Old Law prefigure Christ; the only thing that the New Law prefigures, as distinct from fulfills, is the truth of future glory.

The Old Law contains figures for representing the mystery of Christ; it is a figure of the mystery of Christ.[23] A mystery is something that is kept hidden, or veiled, until it is revealed when the veil is removed. All the sacrifices of the Old Law prefigure the one sacrifice of the Son, who was given to us by God his Father. When we offer sacrifice, we only give back to God what he has given us in the first place. "The immolation of Christ is signified by the sacrifices."[24] The sacrifices of the Old Law were not properly sacraments but only figures of Christ's sacrifice, which *is* a sacrament, because it contains Christ who sanctifies us by his blood (Aquinas alludes to Heb 12:24). And thus this sacrifice is a sacrament.[25] More will be said about how the Eucharist is a sacrifice because it contains Christ in chapter 11. The New Law supersedes the Old, because the Old was only a figure of what was to come. The New Law fulfills what still stands of the Old Law, its moral precepts, and only supersedes what was a figure of the fulfillment, namely its ritual.

Thus, the rites and sacrifices of the Old Law had a twofold purpose: to give worship to God and to prefigure Christ. We can see how the Old prefigures the New Law by the correspondence of the old rites with the sacraments of the New Law.

Old Law	New Law
Circumcision	Baptism
All rites of Purification	Penance (cleanse from sin)
Paschal Lamb	Eucharist
Consecration of priests	Ordination

From this correspondence between the rites of the Old Law and the sacraments of the New we can see that the rites of the Old Law were directed to the sanctification of human beings. But the Old Law was unable to fulfill its purpose, which was to justify people. Its end could only be attained by the New Law, since Christ alone takes away the sin of the world. Although the Old Law could not justify anyone or, therefore, attain its end, it was not useless. On the contrary, St. Thomas agrees with St. Paul in affirming that it was good. He thus refutes the Manichees who rejected the Old Law because they argued that if the Old Law were good, it would be immutable. But since it has been superseded, they denied that it could have come from God. St. Paul affirmed the goodness of the Old Law, calling it "holy, just and good" (Rom 7:12). Commenting on this verse, Aquinas says that it was holy because its ceremonial precepts directed men to the worship of God, it was just because it directed people to their neighbor, and it was good and honest because of its moral precepts.[26] The good aspects of the Old Law were that it taught human beings to recognize their weakness, and so to look to the Mediator of grace by bringing knowledge of sin. It also instructed them about the moral law, which was necessary because reason had been obscured by sin, and it drew them away from idolatry. The sacrifices of the Old Testament directed their minds to God, the source of every good. The rites of the Gentiles were always forbidden by the Old Law, because they were the worship of false gods. Although the rites of the Old Law have now been superseded, they were good because they were ordained by God and prefigured Christ. The Old Law was also good because it brought benefits to Israel. These benefits were the covenant made with Abraham, the worship of God instead of idols, and the promises of future glory. St. Thomas says that these benefits prefigured the spiritual benefits now in operation.[27] But the Old Law was only good for a time, just as the things we have as children are good for their time but do not remain useful later when they have served their purpose. The Old Law "was useful for its time inasmuch as it disposed its recipients for faith."[28] It was good, because it led people to faith in Christ, whom its sacrifices prefigured.

This leads us to the question of whether anyone who lived before Christ could have been justified, as the Old Law was unable to justify. St. Thomas's answer is that, although the Old Law could not itself justify, people under the Old Law were justified by their faith in Christ, but before Christ this faith was in him as he was to come. As we have noted above, St. Thomas regarded some people living under the Old Law as belonging to the New because of charity and the grace of the Holy Spirit. They expressed their faith in Christ by offering the sacrifices, which prefigured him. Although the rites and ceremonies of the Old

Law affected nothing by themselves, they were an indispensable part of being justified by faith in Christ before he came, because they were a profession of faith in Christ, as they pointed toward him. The sacrifices of the Old Law did not take away sin but were an expression of faith in Christ's passion, which does purify us from sin. St. Thomas remarks, commenting on the words "the blood of Christ, who offered himself to God through the eternal Spirit, purifies your conscience" (Heb 9:14), that the blood of Christ purifies us because it was by the prompting of the Holy Spirit, namely by the love of God, that Christ did this.[29] In St. Thomas's view, Christ's blood cleanses us from sin, because he shed it out of love. In the same passage, St. Thomas also remarks that the blood of Christ cleanses, because it was the blood of a lamb without blemish. It was possible, then, for people who lived before Christ to enter heaven not by virtue of the sacraments of the Old Law but by faith in the future Christ, although they did not enter heaven until the gates of heaven had been reopened by the passion of Christ.

To sum up the relation of the Old Law to the New, St. Thomas uses a simile: the New is contained in the Old "as a grain is in the ear of the wheat."[30] The Old Law was good as a tutor until the time when the chosen race could inherit the promise made to Abraham, which was in the singular because it referred to Christ.[31] But the Old Law could not lead anyone to perfection, because only charity makes perfect. Charity, however, belongs to the New Law, because it is poured out by the Holy Spirit, who could only be given by Christ.[32] The moral precepts of the Old Law still stand, and are to be obeyed by everyone; but the ceremonial precepts have been superseded, since Christ's perfect sacrifice replaces all the sacrifices of the Old Law, which pointed toward it. The New Law fulfills the Old, because it justifies by the passion of Christ. As St. Thomas remarks, the Old Law was unable to justify because of the weakness of the flesh; so it was necessary for Christ to be made man in order to accomplish this.[33]

Christ fulfilled the Old Law in two ways: first, he taught by word the original intention of the Old Law, as in the Sermon on

the Mount; second, he fulfilled it by deed, because his passion
has the power to justify us, which is anyway the end of the law.

The Grace of the Holy Spirit

The Old Law gave the precept of charity, as we have noted
above, but it did not bestow the Holy Spirit necessary for having
the charity that is the end of the law. It is only through the Holy
Spirit that the love that fulfills the law is poured into our hearts.
We need charity to keep the commandments, because no one
can keep the law completely without grace, since it is only fulfilled with charity. Charity and grace go together, but they are
not the same. For charity is a virtue, but the root of the virtues is
grace; so grace is prior to charity. But this grace only comes
through Christ, as only he gives the Holy Spirit. Indeed St.
Thomas says that no one ever had the grace of the Holy Spirit
except by "explicit or implicit" faith in Christ.[34] But he taught
that some who lived before Christ had this grace of the Holy
Spirit, because they were more inclined to keep the law by the
eternal promises made to them than by fear. As St. Thomas says
in the preface to question 90 of the First Part of the Second Part
of the *Summa*: "God instructs us by the law and helps us by
grace."

The New Law for St. Thomas is quite simply the grace of the
Holy Spirit.[35] The New Law is the law of the Holy Spirit, because
the Holy Spirit impresses it on the hearts of those in whom he
dwells.[36] The Old Law was engraved on tablets of stone, but the
New is written on the tablets of our hearts. The New Law is more
interior than the Old, because it is implanted in us. Although it
is more interior, it still contains written commandments,
because these dispose us for faith, and the grace of the Holy
Spirit is given to those who have faith. To take an example from
the Sermon on the Mount, the New Law contains written precepts because we are less likely to commit perjury if oaths are
altogether excluded.[37] Moreover, Christ taught the original
intention of the Old Law. The New Law does not just indicate
what is to be done but also gives us the help to keep it. What is
most effective in the New Law, St. Thomas says, is the grace of

the Holy Spirit, which is given us through faith in Christ.[38] The New Law is also more interior, because it brings us grace under the covering of visible signs, by means of which divine power works in us in a more hidden way.[39] These signs are the sacraments of the New Law, which will be our next topic.

10

The Sacrament of Salvation

The sacrament of salvation for St. Thomas is the Cross, from which all the sacraments derive their power. But before we see how Christ achieved the end of the law, which was to justify us, we should give a quick sketch of St. Thomas's view of the Incarnation, for he says that the sacraments are rooted in the Incarnation. St. Thomas regarded the Incarnation as the most wonderful of God's works. As we reveal our thoughts through our outer words, so God has revealed himself through the Word made flesh. Drawing on St. John 14:6 and 6:44, St. Thomas says that we only come to the Father through the Son, and only come to the Son if the Father draws us.

The Incarnation

St. Thomas remarks that there have been two common errors about Christ: one is to say that he was not really human, the other that he was only a man. It is worth noticing that St. Thomas himself held that Christ preached himself to be God.[1] We notice that in his questions on the Incarnation, St. Thomas frequently mentions an error that we hardly consider a major heresy today, namely that of Apollinarius, the Bishop of Laodicea (ca. 310–390). Fergus Kerr, however, points out that this error is still with us and can be found in the works of Karl Barth, who "lays so much emphasis on the unity of the divine and human natures in the person of the Word incarnate that he effectively denied the presence of the human mind or soul."[2] According to Aquinas, Apollinarius followed Arius in holding that the divine Word assumed flesh but not a soul. He tells us that Arius did this so that the things that we cannot say of the body alone, such as fearing and praying, would have to be attributed to the Son of God, who would thus seem to be made less than the Father, as Arius held him to be.[3] Arius conceived the union of body and soul in a human being to be the model of the union of human to divine nature in Christ. Thus, the Word is united to flesh but not to a soul, and the Word takes the place of the soul in this union. Apollinarius, however, differed from Arius by saying that the Word was changed into flesh. St. Thomas points out that if Christ lacked a soul, he was not truly human.[4] Apollinarius later admitted that Christ had a sensitive soul but still held that the Word took the place of the human mind in Christ. But, as St. Thomas is quick to observe, unless Christ had a rational soul, he was not of the same nature as we are. This is against scripture, which says that Christ was sorrowful to the point of death (Mt 26:38), and his soul was troubled (Jn 12:27). Apollinarius's error was firmly excluded by the council of Chalcedon, in 451, which said that Christ is "truly God and truly man, the same of a rational soul and body, consubstantial with his Father in deity, consubstantial with us in our humanity."[5] Thus, Arius and Apollinarius put forward versions of the first kind of basic error about Christ, that he was not really a man. In effect, they confounded the two natures in Christ.

The opposite kind of error was to preserve the natures but to divide the person of Christ. This was what Nestorius, a patriarch of Constantinople, did. St. Thomas says that, as St. John Damascene taught the union in Christ was not according to person (*prosopon*) but *hypostasis* (underlying subject), it appears that

Nestorius said that Christ is one person but two hypostases.[6] Hypostasis is like a subject of action. St. Thomas remarks that if Christ is not one but two, Philippians 2:6–7 becomes meaningless, because it would not be the same person who was in the form of God as assumed the form of a slave.[7] St. Thomas could also point out against Nestorius that if the Word of God only dwelt in the man Jesus as in a temple, scripture would not have said that God emptied himself in taking the form of a slave. It is only when the natures are united in one hypostasis, or *suppositum*, St. Thomas says, that we save what scripture says about the Incarnation, for scripture attributes what belongs to God to a man, Jesus, and what belongs to man to God.[8] Thus, we can say that Jesus has power over nature and God suffered as a man.

St. Thomas explains the difference in meaning between the terms hypostasis and person as follows. A supposit (hypostasis) is an individual existing in nature. Nature signifies the essence of a thing, which the definition of it contains. Person adds nothing to hypostasis except existing in a certain nature, namely in intelligent or rational nature.[9] There is a union of two natures in person and in hypostasis, St. Thomas says, when we are talking of Christ.[10] Arius and Apollinarius held a fusion of natures, and Nestorius a distinction of subjects in Christ. St. Thomas adopted a point secured by St. Cyril of Alexandria in his Third Letter, quoted by the Council of Ephesus in 431: there is one and the same subject of all the things, human and divine, that we ascribe to Christ. The true view is that human nature is united to divine nature in the eternal person of the Word.

St. Thomas clearly held a Christology of descent: a man did not become divine, an error that he attributes to Photius (ca. 810–895), but the Word became flesh. Christ is one person, and this person is the divine Word who has existed from eternity and came down from heaven when he united to himself an individual human nature. For St. Thomas, Christ is not a human person but a divine person who assumed a true human nature (with a human will and a human mind). The divine person already existed; he did not unite a human person to himself, because Christ's human nature never existed by itself but only in union with an already existing person. The divine person is the one subject, or supposit, to which we ascribe human and divine actions in virtue of his two natures, such as thirsting and curing the sick, the first as man and the second because he was God.

As Christ is one person, St. Thomas says that he only has one existence. This view, however, has recently been questioned. Fr. Tom Weinandy, for example, thinks that St. Thomas's real view was that Christ has two existences, although he only once explicitly states this.[11] Aquinas once puts forward the opinion that the person (he says *supposit*) of Christ has "another existence; this existence, however, is not the principal one of his supposit but secondary."[12] Even here he begins his answer by plainly affirming that existence is "properly and truly" predicated of the supposit or subject. He continues: "as Christ is simply one because of the unity of his person, so he has one existence." In the reply to the first objection of this same article, he says, "the existence of divine nature is not the existence of human nature," but in the next sentence adds: "Nor must it be said, however, that Christ is two in his existence." In the *Summa* 3a, 17, 2, he explains that existence belongs to the subject as that which has existence, and to the nature as that by which something exists. He also remarks that Christ would have two existences if human nature were not united hypostatically, that is, in one person, to the Son of God as Nestorius thought. Saying that Christ has one existence seems, then, to go with maintaining the unity of his person; there is one subject of the two natures.

We may sum up some of the main points of St. Thomas's teaching on the Incarnation as follows. First, the Son of God shares in our human nature; he does not come into the world with an already made body from heaven, as the gnostic Valentinus held, or with a phantom body, as the Manichees supposed. Second, Christ shares wholly in our human nature. He did not assume a body without a soul, as Apollinarius at first held, or a soul without an intellect as Arius taught. Third, the Son of God was not related to human nature as God dwelling in a temple, as Nestorius suggested, but human and divine nature were united in one person, so that he who was

God from eternity is also man. There is one supposit, or subject, of the things that Christ did as God and as man. This subject is the eternally existing second person of the Trinity who assumed human nature at the Incarnation. As St. Thomas says, Nestorius was unable to say that this man is the Son of God, because he divided the subjects of action in Christ.

Justification

Quoting Galatians 2:21, "if justification were through the law, Christ died in vain," St. Thomas points out that if people could have been justified under the Old Law, Christ's death was unnecessary. "If this could have been done through the law Christ's death would have been superfluous, but he did not die in vain, because justifying grace and truth came though him alone."[13] It is the same with the sacraments of the New Law: if they can justify us apart from the passion of Christ, his death was also unnecessary.[14] Hence the sacraments derive their power to justify from the Cross. The patriarchs and just of the Old Law were justified by faith in Christ's passion, prefigured by the sacrifices they offered; we are justified by the sacraments that get their power from it.

Justification has two aspects for St. Thomas, which correspond with the death and resurrection of Christ. It not only takes something away by removing sin but also puts something in its place by transforming a person with the gift of new life. The error of Pelagius and Luther was to see only the negative effect of grace taking away sin without the complementary positive effect of transforming a person interiorly. This was like considering Christ's death apart from his resurrection, without which his death would not be fruitful to us. St. Thomas, however, keeps Christ's death and resurrection together, noting, like St. Paul, that we are justified by not only his death but also his resurrection: Jesus our Lord "was handed over to death for our transgressions and was raised up for our justification" (Rom 4:25). Commenting on this verse, Aquinas says:

The death of Christ, by which mortal life was
extinguished in him, is the cause of the extinc-
tion of our sins; but his resurrection, by which
he returns to the new life of glory, is the cause of
our justification, by which we return to newness
of justice.[15]

The death of Christ is the starting point of the movement of
justification, as it removes sin, and the resurrection is the goal of
the movement of crossing over to new life.[16] Thus, Christ's passion justifies us as we are brought from the state of sin, and the
resurrection does so as we are transferred to the new life of grace.

A Sacrifice

St. Thomas makes it clear that the passion of Christ has
power to forgive sins because it is a sacrifice. As all the sacrifices
of the Old Law prefigure the passion of Christ, so his sacrifice
on the Cross united in one the three main types of sacrifices in
the Old Testament: the sin offering, the peace offering, and the
holocaust. Thus, Christ's passion fulfills all the sacrifices of the
Old Testament. Christ's sacrifice of himself was a sin offering,
because it was an expiation for our sins. It was a peace offering,
because it reconciled us with God by taking away the sin that
had made us enemies of God.[17] And it was a holocaust,
because Christ did not offer external possessions to God but his
own life. St. Thomas points out that Christ's sacrifice of himself
was effective where all the previous sacrifices had failed to be,
because God was not pleased with the sacrifices of the Old Law,
as the Old Law itself tells us: "What to me is the multitude of
your sacrifices?" (Is 1:11), and "For you have no delight in sacrifice; if I were to give a burnt offering, you would not be
pleased" (Ps 49:17).[18] The sacrifices of the Old Law, however,
were not worthless, because they at least drew men away from
idolatry and they expressed faith in Christ's passion as it was
still to come. If people were forgiven sin by offering sacrifices
under the Old Law, it was "in virtue of the blood of Christ,

which was prefigured in them."[19] But God was pleased with the sacrifice of his Son, because he came to do his will.[20]

St. Thomas gives three reasons why Christ's sacrifice takes away every sin for all time by a single offering. First, his death was a sacrifice, as he offered his life in obedience to the will of his Father. (Obedience is an interior sacrifice of one's own will.) Second, he was sacrificed as a lamb without blemish, for he was without sin himself. Third, because he was a most pure offering, his blood can cleanse from all sin. Although Christ died out of obedience, he died willingly, because he assumed death by his own will: Christ did not have to die, because he was without sin. Death came into the world through sin (Rom 5:12).[21] Since he offered his life voluntarily he died *out of love* of his Father.[22] This means that Christ could *merit* for us by his death because of the greatness of love that he showed in his passion.

The root of all merit for St. Thomas is charity: our actions only merit eternal life if they are done with charity, which is itself a gift of God poured out in us. Charity was more than abundantly displayed in Christ's passion. St. Thomas draws a link between Galatians 2:20, "he loved me and gave himself up for me," and Ephesians 5:25, "Christ loved the Church and gave himself up for her." He notes that as Christ gave himself up for me, so Christ loved the Church and gave himself up for it.[23] Christ died voluntarily, because he could have eluded his persecutors but instead freely gave himself into their hands. As he died freely, he also merited exaltation and glory.[24] But the rest of the human race only merited death for having been overcome by the Devil in Adam, the root of the whole human stock. Now, however, we are able to merit life through the victory that Christ has gained over death.[25] Christ gained no victory over death unless he rose again, and he did not truly rise from the dead unless he really died. In answer to the question of whether it was fitting for Christ to die, St. Thomas replies: "Fifthly, so that by rising from the dead he would show his power, by which he conquered death, and give us hope of rising from the dead."[26] All this presupposes that Christ assumed a real human nature and that he really rose again in the body that had died. His passion and death only have their power because it was a sacrifice pleasing to his Father.

Christ did not just merit exultation for himself but also for others. His passion is the *universal* cause of salvation, since it takes away the sins of all time. St. Thomas notes that when we are told Christ was slain "from the origin of the world" (Rv. 13:8), this was because he was prefigured in the slaying of Abel.[27] Indeed, as St. Thomas poetically expresses it in the *Adoro te devote*, one drop of Christ's blood would have been sufficient to save the whole world:

> Loving Pelican, Jesus Lord,
> Cleanse me unclean with your blood,
> Of which one drop is able to save
> The whole world from every crime.

The *Adoro te devote* is regarded by Père J. P. Torrell as a genuine work of St. Thomas.[28]

The Grace of Christ

Christ merits for others, since grace was given to his human nature so that it could overflow to others. It was given to him so that it could be "transfused" into others.[29] St. Thomas was of the view that Christ's human nature needed to be raised up by grace just as everyone else's does. The fullness of grace in Christ, however, derives from the immediate union of his divine to his human nature. Grace was not the cause of the union of Christ's human nature to divine nature but an effect that flowed from the union. In other words, Christ did not merit union with the Godhead because of what he did, as though he were first a man raised up to divine status; rather his actions have power to save us because they were done by one in whom divine and human nature are united. A man, Jesus, did not become divine, the view of Photius, but the divine Word who existed from eternity was made flesh. As grace flows from Christ's divine nature into his human nature, through the union of the two in his person, so his humanity is our way to the Father. In order to become partakers of the grace of Christ, we have to be incorporated into the body of Christ. This we are by the sacrament of baptism.

We need to be incorporated into Christ by some tangible sign because, although we all derive from the first Adam by nature, we do not belong to Christ by nature but by grace. As St. Thomas puts it, grace comes to us solely by "the personal action of Christ."[30] Christ pours grace into the members of his body as he is the head of his mystical body, the Church.[31] Head and members, St. Thomas says, make together "as though one person."[32] St. Thomas sees the Church as spanning all time before and after the coming of Christ: her members are united to him from the beginning to the end of time by faith, charity, or glory. Before his coming, his members were joined to him by faith in his future passion; since his coming, they are joined to him by the sacraments in this life; and in the world to come all are joined to him by glory.

Expounding the words "of his fullness we have all received grace upon grace" (Jn 1:18), St. Thomas says that grace is given to us so that we may be joined with God; but of course the kind of union we are capable of having with God differs from the union to divine nature in Christ. We cannot be perfectly joined to God since we do not know him as he is by faith and cannot love him infinitely. But the perfect conjunction of human and divine nature is found in Christ, in whom human nature is united to divinity in a single subject.[33] We come to Christ by believing in him, St. Thomas says, commenting on the words: "No one can come to me unless the Father who sent me draws him" (Jn 6:44). We are drawn to the Son, he says, by love of the Truth, which is the Son of God himself. The Father draws us to the Son "by moving the heart interiorly to believe."[34] Conversely, the Son draws us to the Father by manifesting him. As someone makes known what is secret to him by his word, so no one can come to know the Father except through his Word.[35]

But Christ is the source of grace by his divine and human nature in different ways. His human nature is only the source of grace for us instrumentally, not authoritatively, that is, not as the origin of grace. The sole author of grace is God. The grace

that Christ gives us instrumentally through his human nature
flows from his divine nature as its source. The idea of Christ's
human nature as an instrument of his divinity was taken by St.
Thomas from St. John Damascene.[36] "Since the humanity of
Christ was an instrument of his divinity, as Damascene says, all
the sufferings and actions of Christ's humanity were salutary for
us as they came forth from the power of his divinity."[37] But St.
Thomas is careful to qualify this model, for Christ's humanity is
not like any instrument, such as a chisel or a hammer, since it is
an *animate* one, as Christ's human nature has a human will. St.
Thomas stood firmly behind the teaching of the Third Council
of Constantinople, in 681, that Christ has not one but two
wills, a human one and a divine one. We might be unconvinced
that someone could at once be an instrument yet also act freely,
but there is no contradiction for we commonly see that God
uses people as instruments for his designs, although we think
that they act quite freely in corresponding with the role God
calls them to play. Unless Christ's human nature had a free will
of its own, he did not do anything as man voluntarily, or therefore merit for us, because only what is done voluntarily can be
meritorious.

Similarly, as Christ's humanity is an instrument of his divinity, so the sacraments are instruments of his divine nature,
which perpetuate what God did through his human nature in
healing and restoring people. Divine power works through the
corporeal signs of the sacraments, just as Christ healed the sick
by his divine power through his human actions. The grace that
derives from the Incarnate Word comes to us through the visible
signs of the sacraments, which in their combination of words
and sensible signs reflect the structure of the Word made flesh.[38]
There is a difference, however, between Christ's humanity and
the sacraments as instruments, for his human nature is a *joint*
instrument of his divine nature, being united to it in his person;
but the sacraments are *separate* instruments, as the tools of a carpenter are separate from the carpenter who wields them.[39]

Continuing the Passion

The difference between the sacraments of the Old and the New Law is that the sacraments of the New Law *cause* grace; they do not just signify it but also bring about the effect of grace. The sacraments of the Old Law only signified the grace by which those who lived before Christ were justified. They did this by pointing toward his passion. But the sacraments only cause grace as *instrumental* causes; God remains the sole author of all grace. God achieves the effects he works in us by means of them, just as Christ once wrought miracles by his divine power through the touch of his body. For example, he laid his hands upon the man who first saw people walking around like trees.[40] As Christ's healing actions were a sign of the forgiveness of sins, so forgiveness continues to be worked by the actions of the sacraments. And just as the remission of sin is one of the two main effects of the passion of Christ, so the sacraments are, as St. Thomas says, a "continuation" of his passion.[41] Christ's suffering in the body has spiritual power to forgive sin and heal us, because his humanity is united with his divine nature.

Since Christ's suffering has spiritual power through the union of his human nature with divine nature, so it is effective in us by the spiritual contact we have with God through faith and the sacraments.[42] We "touch" God by faith and the sacraments, St. Thomas frequently says, rather as the woman in the gospel was cured by touching the hem of Christ's garment, because "power went out of him."[43] As Christ worked divine things through his humanity when he touched lepers, so he works spiritual effects through the corporeal elements of the sacraments. "And thus the humanity of Christ is the instrumental cause of salvation; this cause is applied to us spiritually by faith and corporeally by the sacraments, because Christ's humanity consisted of spirit and body."[44] Christ healed with divine power through the actions of his body, and now divine power acts in us through the instrumental causes of the sacraments, which are, as it were, the actions of his mystical body, the Church.

The other main effect of Christ's passion, in St. Thomas's view, was to institute the way we are to worship God, since Christ's perfect sacrifice now supersedes all the rites of the Old Law. The special way we are to worship God, St. Thomas says, is by offering the commemoration of Christ's passion in the Eucharist, when we offer the same victim that was offered on the Cross, namely the body of Christ himself. St. Thomas says of the Eucharist, "We do not offer another sacrifice [hostiam] than that which Christ offered for us, namely his blood. Hence it is not another offering but is the commemoration of that sacrifice which Christ offered."[45] According to St. Thomas, the two main effects of the sacraments of the New Law correspond with the two main effects of the passion, for they either remove the defects of sin through baptism, penance, and anointing of the sick or perfect us for the worship of God through confirmation, marriage, and ordination, leading up to the Eucharist or Mass, which is now the perfect worship of God. "The Eucharist is the perfect sacrament of the Lord's passion, as it contains Christ himself who has suffered."[46] How the Eucharist commemorates the passion of Christ and contains Christ really will be explained more fully in the next chapter.

All Christ's actions are saving for us, because the human nature in which he performed them is united to divine nature in his person. This is especially true of the passion he suffered in his body. Just as grace was given to his human nature for others besides himself, so his actions are effective for others who are related to him as members of his body.[47] What Christ did in his body is not repeated physically in us but done *sacramentally*, that is, by signs. What he did in his body satisfies for the sin of others, since he also merits for the members of his mystical body.

St. Thomas thought that Christ's one sacrifice satisfies for sin in three ways, which correspond with the three main kinds of sacrifice of the Old Law mentioned above: the sin offering, the peace offering, and holocaust. First, Christ paid the penalty of sin—death—by dying. As death comes in through sin, so he satisfies for sin by accepting the penalty of sin and offering his own life, which had that much greater value as it was sinless and perfect. Second, Christ liberates us from sin by making expiation for it. Third, his sacrifice is a peace offering, because he restores peace between the human race and God by taking away the sin that had made us enemies of God. Thus, Christ's passion works by way of *satisfaction* as it liberates us from the guilt of penalty, by way of *redemption* as we are freed from servitude, and by way of *sacrifice* as we are reconciled with God.[48]

Christ's passion is particularly effective in saving us for three further reasons. First, the life he offered to the Father has a greater value as his human nature is united to divine nature in his person. Second, because of the greatness of his charity in giving up his life voluntarily, out of love of his Father. Thus, his sacrifice fulfills all the sacrifices of the Old Law: "The Power of the New Law lies in charity, which is the fullness of the Law."[49] Third, St. Thomas reckons Christ's sufferings were greater than anything suffered by anyone else. Although others have suffered the same torments of crucifixion, even his physical suffering was greater than theirs, because being perfect his human nature was more sensitive. Since he was an entirely innocent victim, his anguish and sense of the injustice done to him made his mental apprehension of the sin that caused it all the greater.

Configured With Christ

Although Christ's passion is the universal cause of salvation, because his one sacrifice is enough to save everyone of all time, it has to be applied to everyone *individually*. "Christ's death is sufficient for saving everyone, but not efficacious for those who are not subject to him by faith and good works."[50] The way we share in Christ's passion, and so in its redeeming effects, is by faith, charity, and the sacraments. Not merely by faith, or unformed faith, but by faith formed with charity, which is the faith of someone who has grace. St. Thomas saw that we share in the virtue of Christ's blood through faith from what St. Paul says: "he (Christ) was presented as a propitiatory sacrifice to be received in faith" (Rom 3:25). This was as true for those who came before Christ as it is for those after him, since people under the Old Law were justified by faith in his passion as it was still to come. But in order to obtain the effects of Christ's passion, we have to be *configured* to it by doing sacramentally what he did in his body, that is, dying and rising again. In baptism we sacramentally die with Christ, and so to sin, and rise to new life in him, by being incorporated into his body. St. Thomas goes so far as to say that when we die with Christ in baptism, it is as though the baptized person suffers and dies.[51] He calls Christ's passion "the sacrament of salvation" (*sacramentum salutis*), because we die to our natural desires and love of self.[52] The Cross is the "sacrament of salvation," because it not only satisfies for sin but also gives us an *example*: first of charity, for no one has greater love than to give his life for his friends; then of courage, which we need to uphold justice, and of patience; and finally of obedience "even unto death."[53]

If one is ever faced with the question why there are just seven sacraments but not all sorts of actions that put us in touch with God in our daily lives are also called "sacraments", one sees from St. Thomas's theory of the sacraments that what distinguishes the seven sacraments of the Church is that they all *apply the passion of Christ* to us in a way that other religious actions and symbols do not. Baptism and penance obviously derive their power from the Cross, because they forgive sin as Christ's passion liberates us from sin.[54] The Eucharist brings us all the fruits of Christ's redeeming death, not just the remission of sin but also the new life he won for us through his death, because it represents the sacrifice of the Cross every time it is offered. The Eucharist is the central sacrament, to which all the other six are directed, because their purpose is either to enable us to receive it by removing sin through baptism, penance, and anointing, to administer it as priests, or to represent the unity it signifies in marriage. Marriage is one of the great sacraments by reason of its meaning, St. Thomas says, because it signifies the union of Christ and his Church.[55] Ordination applies the passion, as Christ showed himself to be our eternal High Priest especially on the Cross. The sacraments apply the effects of Christ's passion to us, because they derive their power from the Cross.

The sacraments work *instrumentally*: like instruments, they get their power from the one who wields them, just as a hammer has no power of its own to beat silver but is an instrument on the hand of the silversmith. The sacraments get their power in the first place from God, because they were instituted by Christ, who is God and man. If there seems to be an exception with confirmation, St. Thomas says that Christ may be said to have instituted this sacrament by promising to send the Holy Spirit. The sacraments are God's instruments for working in us interiorly, because they all come from him. As St. Thomas says, the Church was put together (*fabricata*), literally "woven," out of the sacraments that flowed from the side of Christ on the Cross.[56] Thus, the sacraments that were symbolized by the blood and water flowing from his body on the Cross derive their power from the Cross.[57] But just as Christ entered into his glory through his passion, so we are led to undying glory by first being configured sacramentally with his passion by baptism. We have to be incorporated into his body, in which he died and rose again, in order to die and rise with Christ, so that we may come one day to share his glory.

> Thus as Christ first came by his passion to the glory of immortality, so we too, who are members of him, are set free by his passion and, having been configured with the suffering and death of Christ, are afterwards led into immortal glory, according to what the Apostle says in Romans 8:17.[58]

Our Path to glory in the next life is none other than Christ's: as he had first to suffer to enter into glory, so we have to be configured sacramentally with his passion to reach his glory. Thus, the sacraments, in St. Thomas, are rooted in the Incarnation, which is the source of grace for us, configure us with Christ's passion, and so led us to the new life of the resurrection, the goal of our justification. In the following chapter we shall look more closely at the chief sacrament, the Eucharist.

11

The Eucharist

St. Thomas's writing on the Eucharist appeared in the centuries after him to be so appropriate that by the time of the Council of Trent the Church came largely to adopt his way of explaining it as her own. In recent years, however, there has been a turning away from his approach to the Eucharist because of the Aristotelian terms he uses. We should, however, remember that St. Thomas said that he learned more in prayer before the crucifix at the foot of the altar than he did from books. The primary source of his writing on the Eucharist, then, was not the philosophy of Aristotle but his own devotion to the sacrament, which is admirably expressed in the office he wrote for the feast of Corpus Christi. We know from his biographers that the Eucharist is a topic St. Thomas took the greatest care in writing about. They tell us that on one occasion he anxiously asked Christ whether he had written correctly about him in the sacrament and was told "as far as it is possible for anyone in this life." On another occasion he was asked what he desired as a reward for his labors and replied "Nothing except yourself" (*non nisi te*). The Eucharist is the chief sacrament because, as we have seen, all the others are directed toward it and, unlike the others, it does not just apply to the power of Christ but contains Christ himself, who, as St. Thomas often notes, is "full of grace and truth."[1]

To place the Eucharist in its proper setting, we should first recall that the sacraments of the Old Law pointed toward the passion of Christ. The chief sacrament of the passion in the Old Law, St. Thomas says, was the Paschal Lamb, which directly prefigures the Eucharist, which was itself instituted when Christ was keeping the feast of the Passover at the Last Supper. The sacrifices of the Old Law signified the passion of Christ, but the Eucharist *represents* the passion of Christ.[2] St. Thomas calls it an *imago representativa* (a re-presenting image) of the passion.[3] To re-present is literally to make present again. The Eucharist represents the passion of Christ by its action: first, by the separate consecration of the bread and wine, symbolizing the separation of Christ's blood from his body when he died on the Cross; and second, by the breaking of the host before communion, which represents the breaking of Christ's body in his passion.[4] He left us this way of representing it, St. Thomas says, because no one can be saved without faith in the passion of Christ. Thus, the Eucharist is called a sacrifice, because it represents the passion of Christ. The other two names commonly given to the Eucharist, St. Thomas notes, are "communion," because it signifies the unity of the Church, and "viaticum," because it is spiritual food for us travelers on our way in this life, showing us the way to come to the enjoyment of God in our heavenly homeland. The first question about the Eucharist then is, how does Christ come to be present in this sacrament, and what kind of presence are we talking about?

The very first words of St. Thomas in the *Summa* are: "It must be said that the true body and blood of Christ are (exist) in this sacrament."[5] When St. Thomas says that Christ "really" exists in the Eucharist, he is opposing the view that Christ is in the sacrament merely as a sign, or figure, of his body. The "inventor of this error," he says, was Berengar (ca. 1000–1088), who had been worried that if we eat Christ's body in communion, we bite his flesh with our teeth. In his explanation of the Eucharist, St.

Thomas finds a way of asserting belief that it is the true body and blood of Christ, yet of allaying fear of the consequence that seemed to Berengar to follow from his belief. St. Thomas maintains that the sacrament is the real body of Christ, not just a sign or figure of it, yet we do not bite Christ physically but eat him sacramentally, that is, under the sacramental signs: "the body of Christ is not eaten in its own appearance but in its sacramental appearance."[6] The key to a right understanding of the Eucharist is to keep in mind that the Eucharist, like all the sacraments, is a sign. Yet we have just said that the Eucharist is not merely a sign of the body and blood of Christ, for it is the body and blood of Christ, or contains them. How then is the Eucharist a sign? What is it a sign of, if it is not a sign of Christ's body and blood; or rather, what *are* the signs of this sacrament? It is with the answer to this second question that we come to the heart of the Eucharist.

I take St. Thomas's primary question in his discussion of the Eucharist to be, how does something come to exist where it was not previously? In other words, how do the body and blood of Christ come to be present where there was bread and wine before? He outlines three possible ways by which they could come to be present in the sacrament of the altar: (1) either bread and wine remain with the body and blood of Christ, or (2) the bread and wine are annihilated, or (3) they are *changed* into the body and blood of Christ. This third view is the one that St. Thomas upholds. The first view, that bread and wine continue to exist beside the body and blood of Christ, is known as "consubstantiation." It is the view held by Anglicans and Lutherans. St. Thomas, however, rejects it, because he thinks that it is contrary to the meaning of the words of Christ used at the consecration: "This is my body" and "This is the cup of my blood." If Christ's body and blood were present beside bread and wine, St. Thomas says that we would say, "Here is my Body" rather than "This is my body." Thus, he excludes the view that the substance of bread and wine remain after the consecration, because he says that this would take away "the truth of this sacrament," that the true body of Christ exists in it.[7]

St. Thomas also discounts the second view, that bread and wine are annihilated, and that is how they cease to exist or be present any more after the consecration. Annihilation is the very opposite of creation, which is to make something exist where there was nothing before, since annihilation is to turn something into nothing. But this is not what happens in the Eucharist, because bread and wine are not changed into nothing but into something, namely the body and blood of Christ. So we come to the third view, that Christ's body and blood come to be present where there previously were bread and wine, because the bread and wine that existed there are changed into them.

At the same time as St. Thomas says that there are three things that could happen in the Eucharist, he also says that there are two ways in which Christ's body and blood could come to be present where they were not before. This could either be by local motion, that is, by Christ's body moving from one place to another, or by something being changed into his body and blood. In other words, his body and blood can come to be present where they were not previously either by a change of place or by a change of something into them. St. Thomas rejects the first of these two views, that Christ's body comes to be in the sacrament by moving there, because if it were by movement from one place to another, Christ's glorified body would cease to be in heaven in moving to an altar, and second it could not be on many altars simultaneously, as the end of any movement can only be one place or point. St. Thomas denies that we move the body of Christ when we move the host, since it continues to be at rest in heaven.[8] Thus, he also denies that Christ is present in the sacrament "as in a place," which would be locally, just as he does not come to be present in it by a change of place or by local movement. Another reason why St. Thomas says that Christ is not in the sacrament "as in a place" is that the dimensions of the bread and wine are not changed into the dimensions of Christ's body.[9] The dimensions of the sacramental appearances remain the same, and are just what they appear to be to our sight; but these are not the dimensions of Christ's body in heaven. It is for this reason that St. Thomas says that Christ is present in the sacrament not as in a place but as substance is present. He adopts the view that Christ's presence in the Eucharist is a "substantial" one, because the substance of a thing, what it is, is not affected by its external dimensions. For example, a piece of bread torn from a loaf is just as much bread as the whole loaf is: the piece is the same substance of bread as the entire loaf, although its dimensions are much smaller. But what it is— bread—is just the same.

Connected with this point is another way of describing the presence of Christ's body and blood in the Eucharist: it is a *sacramental* presence, because they are not present in their own appearances, as his body is in heaven, but in the appearances of the sacrament. Thus, it is the *appearances* of bread and wine that are the signs of the presence of his body and blood in this sacrament. This also follows because if the bread and wine are changed so that they are no longer bread and wine, bread and wine cannot anyway be the signs of Christ's body and blood. But the appearances of bread and wine, like their dimensions, remain. *These* then can be the signs of this sacrament, as every sacrament is by its nature a sign. The same body is present in the sacrament as is in heaven, but in a different way: in heaven by its *natural* presence in its own appearance, and here by its *sacramental* presence, that is, beneath the signs of the sacrament. Although the way in which his body is present differs, it is still a real presence in both instances. St. Thomas says that Christ's body can be present in several places at once, in heaven and in the sacrament, because the sacrament has a *relation* to Christ's body, which is not moved every time from heaven to wherever the sacrament is performed but remains in heaven.[10]

This brings us to a further point, which helps us to understand how Christ is present in the sacrament. St. Thomas insists that Christ's body and blood are present *beneath* the sacramental appearances. For example, he explicitly says that the words spoken at the consecration make "what was contained under these appearances, which was bread, the body of Christ." When we say, "This is my body," *this* points to the appearances and says that what is contained by them is the body of Christ.[11] The sense of *this* is that what is contained beneath these accidents, or appearances, is my body.[12] I consistently use the word "appearances" where St. Thomas speaks of the "accidents" of bread and wine, because this makes understanding easier today and has some support from St. Thomas himself, who sometimes uses the word "species" (appearances)—for example, q73:3 and 7 and q.75:3. When we say that the appearances of bread and wine remain the same, although the bread and wine that were there are no longer present but the body and blood of Christ are now present, this can only be so because something has been changed. How this happens will help us to understand how Christ's body can come to be where it was not before, although it does not cease to be in heaven because it is not moved from one place to another. Here we have to return to the third possibility of how something can come to be where it was not previously: by a *change* of what was there previously.

A Supernatural Change

Aristotle remarks that in every change something remains the same and something changes. In any change in nature, there is a change of form, but there is the same underlying matter: for example, when a shell is turned into a fossil. But in the Eucharist we have the opposite, for the outward appearances remain the same but the underlying thing is changed. A natural change is a formal change, that is, a change of form. The change in the Eucharist, however, is not a change of form; rather it is a change of the whole substance of bread and wine. This is so because the appearances of bread and wine do not become the form of Christ's body; rather they continue to exist on their own without inhering in their proper substance. It is here that St. Thomas places the miracle of the Eucharist: the appearances of bread and wine remain in existence without their proper subject or substance. How is this possible? St. Thomas says that they are kept in existence with the existence they previously had in bread and wine, because God continually holds everything in existence anyway.[13]

The change in the Eucharist is also not like a natural change, because bread and wine have no power in themselves to turn into the body and blood of Christ. As bread and wine cannot be changed into Christ's body and blood by any power in nature, the change that occurs in the Eucharist must be above the power of nature, that is, a supernatural one. Thus, St. Thomas says that this change is wrought solely by the active power of God; it is not due to any passive power in bread and wine, as there is a passive power in flour to become bread, and in grapes to be changed into wine.

Since the bread and wine are changed when the words of consecration are spoken over them, we now consider the power of God's word. God's word has a *creative* power: the bread and wine are changed by that word by which all things are created, for the words used at the consecration are the words of Christ himself. The sacrament is "made" by the word of Christ, by whom all things were made. As St. Thomas neatly expresses it: the Word made flesh makes bread be flesh by his word.

> *Verbum caro panem verum*
> *Verbo carnem efficit.*[14]

Since God can make something exist where there was nothing before by his word, as at creation, he certainly has the power to change the whole being of a thing, for he has power over the being of all things, having brought them into existence in the first place.[15] Later St. Thomas quotes the words of St. Ambrose, "If God can bring things into existence out of nothing, he certainly has the power to change the whole being of a thing into another thing."[16] The change effected by the words of consecration is not a formal but a *substantial* one, because the whole being of bread and wine is changed into the body and blood of Christ.

When St. Thomas says that the substance of bread and wine is changed in the Eucharist, he is not dependent on the philosophy of Aristotle, as is often supposed, but is taking up an expression that had already been used by the Church to define her faith about the Real Presence, in the profession of faith drawn up by Gregory VII for Berengar at the synod of Rome in 1079, which said that "bread and wine are substantially changed into the body and blood of Christ." The word "transubstantiate" was used by the Church at the Fourth Lateran Council, in 1215, which was before Aristotle had begun to be used extensively in theology, and also ten years before St. Thomas was born. St. Thomas's point is that the true body and blood of Christ cannot begin to be in this sacrament except by a change of the substance of bread and wine, for it is not a natural change, which would be a change of form, nor does the body of Christ come to be present by a change of its place through moving there.[17]

The bread and wine are changed by the *signifying* power of the words spoken by the priest at the consecration. These words have the power that they do because they are uttered by the priest in the person of Christ. The words have signifying power, because they bring about what they signify, namely that "this is my body" and "this is the cup of my blood." The words are not only significant but also effective (*factiva*), St. Thomas says, because they effect what they signify: they bring about what they say has come about.[18] But the words used do not work just like God's word at creation, for they work *sacramentally*, which is "by the force of signification," as a sacrament is a sign. Thus, the words of consecration are not imperative, as they were at creation ("Let there be light"), but indicative, for they tell us what has come about beneath the sacramental signs.[19]

When St. Thomas answers the question as to why there is no mention of the Eucharist in the Creed, although it is the mystery of faith, he associates it with creation, for he assigns it to the almighty power of God, which has created all things. The Eucharist, however, is both like and unlike creation. It is like creation, because there was nothing with the power to become the world before it was made, just as bread and wine do not have the power to become the body and blood of Christ. Also the change at the Eucharist is not gradual but instantaneous, just as creation happened in an instant: there was nothing, then something. Christ's body is present with the utterance of the final word of "this is my body," and likewise his blood is present beneath the appearances of wine with the completion of the words over the chalice. St. Thomas discourages us from saying that bread "becomes" or "will become" the body of Christ, but allows the expression "become" in the sense that night becomes day, which does not mean that night is made into day, or day is made out of night, but that after night there is day. It is rather of temporal succession: first there is one thing, night or bread, and then there is another, day or Christ's body; after one comes the other.[20] As at creation there first was nothing, then something, so in the Eucharist there is bread, then the body of Christ.

But the change in the Eucharist is also *unlike* creation, because it is a change, whereas creation was not the change of anything that was there before, for there was nothing to be changed until something had been created. Creation was bringing about that there was something where there had been nothing. St. Thomas calls the change of bread and wine into the body and blood of Christ a "conversion," but creation was not the change, or conversion, of non-being into being. We may note that he uses the word "conversion" rather than "mutation," since conversion suggests a more deeply rooted, or total, change, such as occurs in the Eucharist.

The change in the Eucharist is a unique kind of change, for it is not a natural one but "brought about solely by the power of God." The whole substance of bread is changed into the whole substance of Christ's body, and the whole substance of wine is changed into the whole substance of Christ's blood. Nothing remains of bread and wine except their appearances: "After the consecration nothing remains beneath the appearances of the sacrament but the body and blood of Christ."[21] Christ's presence in the Eucharist is a substantial one, because he is present in the way that substance is present.[22] First, as we saw with the example of the loaf and a part of it, the substance of a thing, what it is, is wholly present in every part. Also, as we have seen, substance is not varied by the size or dimensions of a thing. St. Thomas says that Christ is present in the sacrament "in the way that substance is" (*per modum substantiae*), to contrast this with being as in a place, which is with measurable dimensions.[23]

"But it is clear the nature of a substance is whole under any part of the dimensions under which it is contained."[24] When he says that Christ is not in the sacrament as in a place, he means that he is present not with the dimensions of his body but as substance is present. Christ is present in this sacrament not with his own appearances but with sacramental appearances, that is, beneath the appearances of bread and wine. As the Dominican writer Colman O'Neill explains, "Substances permits us to state that a thing is either bread or the body of Christ and that a thing understood in this way cannot be both bread and the body of Christ simultaneously."[25] Seen in this way, the use of the word "substance" is connected with establishing the real presence of Christ in the Eucharist, and that it is his true, or real, body and blood. For whatever the sacrament is, it cannot *really* be both together: it can only really be the body of Christ or bread. This only draws out what is implied by the words "this is my body." If it were both, side-by-side, as held by the view of consubstantiation, one would have to say, "This bread is my body." But, as it is, "this" is only said to be one thing, the body of Christ. St. Thomas says that "this" (*hoc*) signifies the substance contained beneath the accidents, which was first bread and is afterward the body of Christ.[26]

The Eucharist is the sacrament of the *humanity* of Christ; we do not need a sacrament of his divinity, for God is everywhere. But the whole Christ is present in the Eucharist. This is because what is joined in reality is not divided in the sacrament. As human nature continues to be united to divine nature in the person of Christ, so where his body and blood are present there also is his soul, which is a part of his true human nature, and his divinity, which is united to his human nature. The presence of his body and blood in the sacrament is itself evidence of the resurrection, because by his resurrection his body and soul, which were separated at death, were reunited. His soul is always united to his body in reality, because Christ rose from the dead, to die no more.[27] Thus, the *whole* Christ is present in the sacrament.[28] "The whole Christ exists in this sacrament," because (1) his body and soul were rejoined at his resurrection when his body was raised to life again, and (2) he is present by way of substance, which is wholly in every part. But his body and blood are present in different ways beneath the sacramental appearances of bread and wine. His body is present by "the power of the sacrament" beneath the appearances of bread, for they are the sign of his body, but by "natural accompaniment" beneath the appearances of wine, as his body and blood go together in reality. You cannot have his body without his blood, just as you cannot have a pound of flesh without a drop of blood in it. Conversely the blood of Christ is present by "the power of the sacrament" beneath the appearances of wine, for these are the sacramental sign of his blood, and by "natural accompaniment" beneath the appearances of bread. Soul and divinity are present, St. Thomas says, because the divinity has never discarded the body and soul it assumed by the Incarnation; so it exists wherever Christ's body does.[29]

Effects and Benefits

Throughout his work St. Thomas keeps in view two aspects of the Eucharist: (1) it is a sacrifice, as it represents his passion, and (2) it gives us a share in the life of Christ. From these two aspects flow the five effects, or benefits, that its reception produces in us. First, since "this sacrament is nothing other than the application of the Lord's passion" to us, we receive all the benefits of his redeeming death from it. "Hence it is clear that the destruction of death, which Christ destroyed by dying, and the reparation of life, which he effected by rising again, are the effect of this sacrament."[30] It is because his body was raised to life again that it can be life-giving for us now. Christ as man receives life from the union of his human to his divine nature, and we share in this life by partaking of his body and blood in communion. St. Thomas quotes the scriptural basis for this parallel way in which Christ draws life from his Father and we from him: "As the living Father sent me, I too live through the Father, and whoever eats me will also live through me."[31]

The second effect of the Eucharist is that it refreshes our spiritual life. The Eucharist is *spiritual* food. We need food for our spirit, as we need food for the life of the body. St. Thomas says that we cannot sustain our spiritual life without it.

Third, by the Eucharist we participate in the unity of the Church, which is the mystical body of Christ. As St. Thomas notes, "The Eucharist is especially the sacrament of unity and charity."[32]

Fourth, it works in us the resurrection: as Christ's body was raised up to life again, so whoever shares in his body will be raised up again.[33]

This leads us to the fifth effect, which is that the Eucharist brings us to glory. Just as the priests of the Old Law had to enter the Holy of Holies once a year through the veil of the Temple, so we enter into glory through the flesh of Christ, which is the veil of his divinity. Commenting on "the new and living way which he (Jesus) has opened up for us through the veil, that is, through his flesh," St. Thomas writes: "His flesh is given under the veil of the appearances of bread in this sacrament."[34] Christ presents his body in the Eucharist in an invisible way that is discerned by faith. As St. Thomas says in the *Adoro te devote*: "On the cross only his godhead was hidden, but here his humanity is also at the same time." It was ever St. Thomas's prayer that one day he would come to see revealed face-to-face what he received here on earth veiled in the Eucharist.

> Jesus, whom I now behold veiled,
> I pray that come about for which I so thirst:
> That seeing you with face unveiled
> I may be blessed with the sight of your glory.[35]

Thus, St. Thomas also calls the Eucharist "the bread of angels" (*panis angelorum*), because just as the good angels feed their minds on the continual vision of the Word, so we will feed on the same vision in heaven.[36]

12

The Resurrection

In the previous chapter we saw that the Eucharist presupposes the resurrection, because Christ's body is not life-giving unless it has been raised up again. It may, therefore, be useful to set forth in order what St. Thomas says about the resurrection of the dead, especially in his commentaries on scripture. St. Thomas defines resurrection as "the restoration from death to life." He also calls it a "re-integration." The first point that St. Thomas makes is that Christ's resurrection is the cause of our resurrection, because he was the first to rise from the dead. Although others were raised to life again before him—for example, the only son of the widow—Christ was the first to rise from the dead without being subject to the necessity of dying. For support, St. Thomas quotes 1 Corinthians 15:20, "Christ has been raised from the dead, the first fruits of those who have fallen asleep." The first cause of the resurrection, St. Thomas says, is the justice of God, by which Christ is given power to judge as the Son of man.[1] Christ's resurrection is the secondary cause of our resurrection. Quoting John 5:21, "As the Father raises up the dead and vivifies them, so the Son also vivifies whom he wills,"

St. Thomas says that Christ is the cause of the resurrection by the power of the divine Word united to his body and soul.[2] Christ is the efficient and exemplary cause of the resurrection. He is the efficient cause through his humanity, which is an instrument of his divinity. As Aquinas says, Christ is the exemplar and efficient cause of our resurrection in virtue of his divinity through his humanity, as it is an instrument of his divinity.[3] Thus, he is the efficient cause by his divine power, to which vivifying the dead belongs. Quoting 1 Corinthians 15:12, "if Christ has been raised from the dead, how can some of you say there is no resurrection of the dead?" he makes the point that our resurrection does not follow logically from Christ's, but says it is better to say "because Christ's resurrection is the cause of ours."[4] Christ's resurrection is also the exemplary cause of our resurrection, for our resurrection will be modeled on the pattern of his, when our lowly bodies will be configured with his glorious body (Phil 3:21). But St. Thomas qualifies this by saying that it is only the exemplary cause of the resurrection of the good, not of the bad, but the efficient cause also of the resurrection of the evil.[5] In one place St. Thomas adds that Christ's resurrection is the exemplar of ours *sacramentally*; we are conformed with Christ's suffering and dying in this life through the sacraments, and then we shall come to participate in the likeness of his resurrection. St. Thomas quotes Romans 6:5, "if we had been united with him in a death like his, we shall be united with him in a resurrection like his," where St. Paul talks about being buried with Christ in baptism.[6]

St. Thomas believed completely in the reality of Christ's resurrection in the body: Christ showed that he had risen from the dead, he says in Acts 1:3, "by many signs," to manifest the truth of his resurrection. Christ also "proved his resurrection by the authority of sacred Scripture, which is the foundation of faith."[7] Christ appeared to certain people to show that he had risen, but he only did this at intervals, to let them know that he was now in another kind of life, no longer subject to death. A glorious body has the power to be visible and invisible, to be seen in its natural color or in glory, because it is subject to the spirit. It was in Christ's power, Aquinas says, to let his body be seen in its color without glory.[8] The Apostles knew that Christ had truly risen, since the scars of his wounds showed that he had numerically the same body, as St. Luke indicates: "Touch, see, my hands and my feet, that it is I myself."[9] As St. Thomas several times says, the same body rose as died on the Cross, because the same body rose as was buried: "Numerically the same body of Christ was nailed to the cross and lay in the tomb."[10]

St. Thomas remarks that there are two errors about the resurrection: one is to deny it; the other is to say that there is only a spiritual resurrection but no future resurrection of the body. Those who say there is only a spiritual resurrection, like Philetus and Hymenaeus, "destroy the foundation of the faith."[11] There is a double resurrection, St. Thomas affirms, as there is a double death: of body and of soul (the second is a spiritual death). He points to the distinction of resurrections in the Gospel of St. John: first, it says the dead will hear the voice of the Son of God and those who hear will live (5:25). This is a spiritual resurrection in this life. Then it says that "all who are in the tombs will hear his voice and come forth, those who have done good, to the resurrection of life, and those who have done evil, to the resurrection of judgment" (5:28–29). St. Thomas remarks that Jesus adds "in the tombs" because souls are not in tombs but bodies are. Thus, the second saying refers to the resurrection of the body in the future.[12]

St. Thomas thought that belief in the immortality of the soul leads to belief in the resurrection of the body. Since the human soul is by its nature the form of the body and it can be shown that it is immortal, as we saw in chapter six, but nothing contrary to nature can remain forever, the soul must be reunited with the body. "The immortality of the soul seems to demand the future resurrection of bodies."[13] Aquinas also argues that, since the soul is a part of human nature and everything naturally desires perfection, we cannot have perfect felicity unless the soul is rejoined to the body. He thought that, as we have a natural desire for the resurrection, if there is no resurrection a natural desire would be frustrated, for we naturally desire our salvation;

but the soul is not the whole human being. As Aquinas famous-
ly says, "If only my soul is saved, I am not saved, nor is any other
human being."[14] Thus, he thought desire for the resurrection of
the body to be implicit in the desire to be immortal. As he says,
the soul naturally desires to be united with its body.[15] It was seeing that it would be against nature for souls to be perpetually
separated that followers of Plato supposed that they are put
back into bodies by reincarnation. "If resurrection of the body is
denied, it is not easy, nay it is difficult to uphold immortality of
the soul."[16] But St. Thomas argues against reincarnation, for our
resurrection will be on the pattern of Christ's, but Christ rose
again to die no more. Conversely, if the dead do not rise again,
our hope is only for this life, for the soul cannot exist on its own
forever, as our nature would remain incomplete forever. St.
Thomas would say that from the point of view of the end, the
resurrection is natural, since it is natural for the soul to be
reunited with the body; but it is not natural from the point of
view of its active source, which is divine power alone.

What Sort of Body?

Two questions readily arise about the resurrection: *What sort*
of body will we have when we rise again? And will it be the *same*
body that is raised up? St. Thomas's answer to the first of these
questions was that it will be a body of the same nature but in a
different state. To illustrate this, St. Thomas uses the analogy of
stained glass, which is dull and opaque from the outside but brilliant inside with sunlight streaming through it, though it
remains matter of the same nature.[17] He quotes St. Gregory the
Great (Homily on the Gospel 26): "a body of the same nature
but different glory." We shall not rise as spirits but with a spiritual body, he says, just as now we are not souls but animals; commenting on 1 Corinthians 15:46: "first comes the natural
[*psuchikon*, literally "the ensouled"]. Then comes the spiritual."[18]
We shall not be pure spirit, like the angels, but have a spiritual
body. A spiritual body is one that is wholly subject to the spirit,
but it is still a body. St. Thomas explains that, as the body is
moved by the desire of the soul, so the risen bodies of the blessed

will totally obey the soul that has reached the fulfillment of its desires. The body will also be spiritual because its activities will no longer serve the body but unceasingly serve the soul. As St. Thomas says, "The body of someone rising will be spiritual, not because it is a spirit . . . but because it will be altogether subject to the spirit."[19] If we do not rise with a body of the same nature, he retorts, we will only be human beings equivocally, since we shall not be the same species as now. Unless I am the same species, I shall not be the same human being or person.[20]

He argues that the resurrected body will be of the same nature, though have different qualities, just as the body in this life remains the same kind of body although it passes through different stages from conception to maturity and thence to old age. Commenting on St. Paul's comparison of the differences between the earthly and risen body with the difference between the seed that is sown and the fully grown blade, St. Thomas compares the sowing of the seed with the laying of the body in the tomb.[21] As he points out, St. Paul uses this analogy not to show that the resurrection is natural but to show that the quality of the risen body will be different. He notes a further difference: the body is generated by the active power of the seed, but the dust into which the body dissolves has no power of its own to rise again. The sole cause of the resurrection, therefore, is the power of God. Another difference, St. Thomas notes, is that what grows from the seed is not numerically the same individual, only of the same kind, whereas the body that rises is numerically the same but with a different quality. He also notes that nature only perpetuates the species with new individuals, but God can also make the individual perpetual; to perpetuate the individual belongs to a power that surpasses nature.[22]

The four special qualities of the risen body, according to St. Thomas, are impassibility, clarity, agility, and subtlety. He derives these qualities from St. Paul's list of contrary qualities: "What is sown corruptible is raised incorruptible; what is sown in dishonor is raised in glory; what is sown in weakness is raised in power; what is sown a physical (ensouled) body is raised a spiritual body" (Cor 15:42–44). St. Thomas discountenances the idea that subtlety enables a risen body to be in the same place as another body. When Christ entered the room through closed doors, this was not due to a property of his risen body, St. Thomas says, but due to the divine power united to his body.[23] Only glorious bodies are impassable, he says, but the bodies of the damned will suffer. Thus, the risen bodies of the blessed and damned will differ in quality.

St. Thomas thought that all these errors were excluded by the Book of Job 19:26–27: "then from my flesh I shall see God, whom I shall see on my side, and my eyes shall behold and not another." He says that the risen body will be capable of touch (*tactivum*), since there is no animal without touch. He even thinks the blessed will enjoy delight of the senses that are not incompatible with the state of incorruption.[24] Being impassable does not mean being insensible. As Christ rose with a palpable body, St. Thomas says, quoting Luke 24:39, "touch me and see, for a spirit has not flesh and bones as you see that I have," others too will rise with palpable bodies "composed of flesh and bones," for our bodies will be conformed with Christ at the resurrection.[25] Christ's body was palpable since he offered it to be touched when he entered through closed doors, but it was not corruptible, because the glory that flowed into it from his soul rendered it incorruptible.[26] Coining the word *Christiformis*, Aquinas says that the resurrection will make us "Christ-shaped," because not only will the soul be beatified but the body, in its way, will be glorified, too.[27]

St. Thomas argues that the body too will share in the soul's vision of God after the resurrection. As the souls of the blessed are lifted up by clarity, or glory, and power to have the vision of God, so the bodies joined to them will be lifted up by clarity. The spiritual clarity of the soul will flow back into the body. For this he uses the word *redundantia*, which suggests a wave going back into the waves following it. As St. Thomas says, it is the soul that gives the body its existence, its beauty, clarity, and agility.[28] Agility comes from the body obeying the soul with ease.

It is clear that, in St. Thomas's view, the properties of a risen, glorified body do not so much derive from a physical transformation of matter as from the glory of the soul that enjoys the vision of God. As a soul is lifted up to a glory surpassing its natural power in that blessed vision, so the risen body will surpass the natural perfection of the heavenly bodies, St. Thomas says, by its greater brightness (*claritas*), its stronger impassibility, easier agility, and more perfect dignity of nature.[29] Commenting on the passage of Job quoted above, and counteracting in advance Descartes' view that a mind rather than a human being thinks, St. Thomas affirms that not just the soul but the human being will have the vision of God: "not only my soul will see God but I myself, who consists of body and soul." But the eyes of the body will not have quite the same vision as the soul does. The body will participate in the vision of God in its own way, St. Thomas says, not that the eyes of the body will see the divine essence but they will see God made man. The eyes of the body will see the glory of God shining in the creature. The flesh will be no barrier to seeing God after the resurrection, St. Thomas observes, contrary to what the followers of Plato thought.[30]

St. Thomas goes on to note that in 1 Corinthians 15:42–50, St. Paul shows that what was animal will be raised up spiritual because the human race has two sources, the one natural, the other through grace: namely, Adam and Christ, the last Adam, as St. Paul calls him. Adam is only a living soul, but Christ is a life-giving spirit through his divine nature. Adam was taken from the earth, Christ came down from heaven in his divine nature, not because he brought a body from heaven, for he assumed this from the Virgin, but because the divine nature that was united to it came down from heaven. Adam is the principle of our natural life and animal nature; Christ is the principle of our spiritual life and grace.[31] The last Adam, Christ, is said by St. Paul to have a heavenly body, St. Thomas explains, not because he brought it from heaven, for he derived it from the Virgin Mary, but because divine power is united to it, and it is now an immortal and spiritual body. Aquinas says that we are conformed with the heavenly man by the life of grace, which leads us to the life of glory. The risen body will be celestial not in nature but in glory.[32] Now we bear a likeness to the heavenly man by grace and so come to the life of glory. When St. Paul says that flesh and blood will not possess the kingdom of God (1 Cor 15:50), Aquinas says that he does not mean that we will not have bodies in heaven but is referring to those who live carnally now. St. Thomas deemed it an error to think that we shall have ethereal or celestial bodies in heaven; they will be bodies of the same nature. He would not have thought that we shall have "stellar" bodies, as it has been quite popular to suppose in the modern world.

Will It Be My Body?

God raises up not just bodies of the same kind (of the same species) but the numerically identical individuals as lived in this world. How can he raise up numerically the same body so that it will be *my* body? If the resurrection were natural, St. Thomas says, numerically the same body could not be raised up, as we have already mentioned; but the resurrection comes from another source—the glory of the soul. "In the resurrection numerically the same soul will return, since it is incorruptible, and the same body in number will be restored by divine power from the dust into which it has dissolved, so that numerically the same human being will rise again."[33] The same body can be corruptible and incorruptible, just as the same will in nature and number is variable in this life but fixed in its ultimate choice in the next.

On the question of whether the same material constituents as the body had in this life will be required for the same body to be raised up, St. Thomas answers with the help of an analogy: it does not need to be exactly the same matter for the same human being to rise again, just as a fire remains the same fire although the logs are consumed and new ones are added. "Thus for numerically the same human being to rise again it is not required that anything that was materially in him for the whole time of his life be resumed, but only as much as it suffices to complete the right quantity."[34]

To sum up: Our resurrection will be like Christ's, which is both the cause and the pattern of ours. Christ showed that he had really risen from the dead with a palpable body. The resurrection is not just spiritual in this life but there is still a bodily resurrection to come at the end of time. The body that is raised up will be of the same nature but in a different state for the blessed in glory. God does not just raise specifically the same kind of beings but the numerically identical individuals as were in this life. This is not possible by nature but only by divine power.

13

Charity and Friendship

It is appropriate that we come to charity last of all. First, because love is of the good and only the good can be an end. Charity is the love of God, who is the highest good and end of all things. Second, because however much St. Thomas may appear to emphasize the role of the intellect at the expense of the heart in religion, he gives the final word to love, for he says that the intellect's knowledge is only completed by love. With the intellect we apprehend our end, but the will inclines us toward it. However much reason may lead us to know about God as the cause of all things, St. Thomas thought that we come to God more as we are drawn by love. "Man is more able to tend to God by love as he is passively drawn by God himself than his own reason can bring him to this."[1]

St. Thomas distinguishes between love (*amor*) and charity (*caritas*). All charity is love, but not all *amor* is charity: the difference between the two is that love is of what is wanted as good for me, but charity is love of what is wanted as good for the other.[2] Love (*amor*), as we saw in chapter 7, is an emotion; charity is a virtue. Love may or may not be of something according to reason. Love is natural; charity is a supernatural or infused virtue. James McEvoy suggests that Aquinas bridges the gap between love (*amor*) and charity by employing the notion of friendship.[3]

Much of St. Thomas's teaching about the virtues is based on Aristotle. When he came to charity, however, St. Thomas could find no equivalent virtue in Aristotle, because Aristotle does not include love among the virtues in the *Nicomachean Ethics*. For Aristotle the virtue is friendship rather than love, because virtue is by definition a settled disposition for him and friendship requires a more permanent relation; but he regards love as an emotion rather than a virtue, as it appeared to be of a transitory nature. Aristotle counts friendship as a virtue (it is the only virtue to which he devotes not just one but two books of the *Nicomachean Ethics*), because being friends with others involves the practice of all the virtues. As McEvoy points out, St. Thomas was also moved to discuss charity in terms of friendship by the Gospel of St. John: "I no longer call you servants but friends."[4]

We are used to thinking of friendship as one of the forms of love (C. S. Lewis counts it as one of the four loves with affection, eros, and charity), but for St. Thomas friendship is not a kind of love; rather charity is a kind of friendship. As he presupposes Aristotle's description of friendship in his treatment of charity, it will be helpful here to give a brief account of Aristotle's view of friendship, with the help of St. Thomas's commentary on this part of the *Ethics*. This will also help us better appreciate how charity differs from merely natural virtue.

Aristotle on Friendship

For Aristotle, friendship is part of happiness (*eudomonia*, or human flourishing and well-being), because it is characteristic of human beings to act for an end and our end, he says, is happiness, because this is what everyone desires. With wealth, honor, health, and wisdom (or knowledge), friendship was counted by the ancients as one of the things that bring us most happiness. But Aristotle notes that no one would want any one of these other things without friends with whom to share it.

What are all the possessions or works of art I could want if I am without friends? We need friends whether in prosperity, because possessions are little to us if we have no friend with whom to enjoy them, or in adversity, because friends are our only refuge in adversity.

Aristotle says that there are three kinds of friendship: the useful, the pleasant, and the honorable. I can be a friend to someone merely for the sake of utility: for what I can get out of the other person or we can obtain together to our mutual advantage. Friendship among acquaintances in business or in politics and diplomacy may be of this kind. This is friendship based on self-interest and profit. Then people can be friends for the sake of pleasure and of enjoying some activity together: it may be playing music or going to concerts or playing tennis together. The third kind of friendship is loving the other person for what he or she is, for the sake of the other. Aristotle thought that only friends of this third kind are truly friends, and Aquinas that only this kind can be perfect friendship.

In St. Thomas's view, perfect friendship exists for the good of virtue.[5] As one can only love others for their own sake because of what is good in them, the third kind of friendship can only exist between good or virtuous people, for only good people can be delightful to one another. A friend is someone who pleases one, he says.[6] Bad people can be friends for the sake of utility, for example, crooks; but they cannot be friends in the third way, the honorable. For this kind of friendship one needs to have experience of the friend for a long time. The other kinds of friendship, the first and second, can be formed more quickly and often do not last so long. St. Thomas notes that friendship "is the most generous, inasmuch as friends are loved for the sake of themselves."[7]

The third kind of friendship, for the sake of the other, is the truest kind of friendship, because it implies possession of the other virtues, which are settled dispositions of character. Bad people do not possess the constancy required for true friendship, for they are often inconsistent in themselves. Not only do we require virtue to be friends with others in the truest way but we also require friends, Aristotle notes, in order to acquire and exercise the virtues that this kind of friendship presupposes. We cannot, for example, be generous without others. St. Thomas says that friendship provides the occasion for practicing the other virtues: for example, compassion and benevolence. Moreover, good people become even better, and thus more lovable for what they are in themselves, by exercising the virtues in company with others. The virtuous person, in St. Thomas's eyes, is someone who orders his or her affections to their proper end.

Friends bring one another mutual benefits in good or bad times. No one can do without friends, because they are our only support in good and bad times. We need friends with whom we can share our sorrows, for no one can bear sorrow alone for a long time, Aristotle observes.[8] For a similar reason, St. Thomas notes, we cannot persevere in virtue unless we delight in it, because we cannot bear for long what grieves, or sorrows you. In good times, on the other hand, the company of friends is part of the good life, as it is pleasant and agreeable. A friend's happiness adds to one's own, just as sharing a sorrow with a friend lessens it (as we saw in chapter 7, about the remedies for sorrow). Nothing is as characteristic of friends, Aristotle notes, as spending time together.[9] The mere presence of the other makes one happy; friends find one another's company delightful. A property of friendship, St. Thomas remarks, is to rejoice in one another. Thus, special causes of friendship are conversation, which may also mean a shared life in community, and concord, by which he means the agreement of emotion in sharing one another's joys and sorrows. "Thus the principle act of friendship," St. Thomas says, "is to live with a friend."[10] The mark of a friend, for St. Thomas, is that he or she (1) wants his or her friend to live, (2) wishes good things for the other, (3) does good things for the other, (4) finds a common life with the other delightful, and (5) is of one heart (in concord) with the other, rejoicing and sorrowing about the same things. From this we see that friendship includes goodwill, generosity, companionship and conversation, concord and sympathy.

In Aristotle's opinion, we cannot be friends to others unless we are first a friend to ourselves. Just as the Great Commandment of the New Law, quoting the Old Law, says "love your neighbor as yourself,"[11] which requires that we love ourselves as well as others, so Aristotle too thought that friendship presupposes love of oneself. We will not be friendly to others unless we are friendly to ourselves, for "a person extends to his friends the same relation that he has to himself. . . . The friendly feelings we have towards our neighbors seem to derive from our feelings towards ourselves."[12] But only good people can truly love themselves with a love of self that is not selfish. Bad persons are not disposed as friends to themselves, because their desires conflict. Good persons have true love of self; bad persons have rather self-interest as their aim. For Aristotle, we love ourselves when we love the good of the higher part of our nature, which is reason. This most of all seems to be ourselves, he says, because it controls the emotions. A good person loves reason, because reason is the individual self.[13] This love of self, however, is directed to others in Aristotle, for he says that good persons should love themselves as this includes having a care for fine actions, which will benefit society. Fine actions for Aristotle are virtuous actions, like acts of generosity and magnanimity. In this respect, good persons are not the ones with less love of self but who love themselves *more*, because they love the good of their rational nature. The greatest of goods, Aristotle says, is virtue.[14] But for St. Thomas our spiritual good is higher than the social good of friendship.

St. Thomas describes the qualities of proper love of self in a passage reminiscent of Aristotle, *Ethics* book IX, chapter 4:

> Good people love themselves in the inner person, since they want to preserve their integrity and they desire spiritual things. They set themselves to attain these and they return to the heart with delight, because they find there good thoughts in the present, the memory of good things in the past, and hope of good things to come, which brings them delight. They suffer no

> dissension of the will in themselves, because
> they tend with all their soul to one end. But bad
> people, on the contrary, do not want to keep
> their integrity, nor seek spiritual things . . . nor is
> it delightful for them to return to their heart,
> because they are not at peace (non-concordant)
> on account of their gnawing conscience.[15]

Aristotle too had noted that virtuous persons are completely integrated in themselves, because they have no conflicting desires. He goes on to remark that for good persons, their own existence is desirable: they like their own company, have entertaining memories, and have minds furnished with topics for contemplation.[16] Virtuous persons, St. Thomas remarks, have concord, because they are not led by passion to do anything against reason. Thus, to love reason, the higher part of ourselves, is also to love virtue. In St. Thomas's view, the lower, corporeal, and sensitive part of our nature should serve the higher part. It is the lower part that bad people love first. For St. Thomas, all nature is ordered, and virtue lies in keeping this order.

As one's own existence is desirable in itself to the good person, and what makes one's existence desirable in itself is the consciousness of one's own goodness, we may wonder whether the virtuous person needs friends in order to be happy. It seems that integrated persons who can enjoy their own company because they have pleasant memories and their minds are filled with thoughts are self-sufficient and, therefore, no longer need friends. Aristotle's *Ethics* indeed contains an inconsistency, which he never resolves, for in the first book he says that we need the society of friends in order to acquire and exercise the virtues, which bring us happiness. But in the last book, he says that happiness lies in an activity, for it is activity that perfects the power of any nature; and that activity that is most like God's will make us most happy. This is contemplation. But the exercise of contemplation does not require the company of friends, since it is something done by oneself. Here we see how Aristotle's dilemma is resolved by the Christian doctrine of the communion of the saints. Commenting on the last article of the Apostle's Creed concerning eternal life, St. Thomas says that part of our happiness in heaven, which he regarded as consisting in the vision or contemplation of God face-to-face, will be to delight in friends who share in the same beatitude that comes from contemplating God.

> Fourthly, it (eternal life) consists in the joyful society of all the blessed. This society will be especially delightful, because everyone will share in all good things with all the blessed. For everyone will love the other as himself, and so will rejoice in the good of the other as his own. By this it comes about that the gladness and joy of one is increased as much as the joy of all.[17]

Since the blessed are self-sufficient, for their happiness comes from an activity that does not require others, they do not need useful friends; but they still need delightful friends, for their company is part of what makes life delightful. Not only do the blessed have the joy that comes from sharing all the good things that the others possess, but their happiness in heaven will be that much greater, St. Thomas says, as they will love others perfectly.

Aristotle, however, has nothing like the love of God, which is what charity properly is, in all that he says about friendship. He goes no higher than friendship among human beings. Indeed, Aristotle thought that as friendship requires a certain equality, friendship between God and human beings is not possible because the distance between them is too great.[18] St. Thomas, however, says that the gap has now been bridged by the Incarnation, since God's own Son shares in our human nature, which is made in the image of God. Aristotle thought that our highest happiness lies in contemplation, for this is most like God's activity, but he does not associate this with the love of God. For the Christian, however, ethics is not just about the noble life, as it was for Aristotle, but about friendship with God.

Charity

St. Thomas also overcomes Aristotle's difficulty about the lack of equality between God and human beings by saying that friendship is founded on sharing something. We can have friendship with God because it is founded on sharing in his own blessedness or beatitude. Thus, the friendship of charity has a foundation and an end; indeed, the foundation of our friendship with God is also its end, because the beatitude it is founded on is our final end. We cannot reach this end without charity, for we can only be made happy or blessed by something that we love. St. Thomas notes that charity loves the good, which is shared in by the saints. "Charity is itself the communication in the spiritual life, by which we come to blessedness."[19] We cannot have charity, however, without grace, because it is founded on something that we can only share as a gift from God, and the love of a good that is above nature, such as God's blessedness, is something above our natural powers; so it can only be obtained by grace. Thus, charity is a supernatural virtue, both because of its object and the way it comes to be in us.

For St. Thomas, charity is both God's love of us and our love of God.

> But the charity (love) of God can be taken in two ways. In one way as the charity by which he loves us; in another way the charity of God can mean the love by which we love God. But both kinds of charity of God are poured into our hearts by the Holy Spirit who has been given to us.[20]

As St. Thomas notes, following St. Augustine, God does not love us because we love him; rather by loving us first, God makes us lovers of himself. "For God makes us lovers of himself by loving us, according to Proverbs 8:17: I love those who love me; not as though they loved first, but because he makes them lovers by loving them."[21] St. Augustine points out that we are not given grace because we love God, but grace makes us lovers of God in the first place.[22]

Charity orders all the other virtues to their end, since it directs us to God, who is our final end. By charity, St. Thomas says, we love God above all things and refer everything else to him.[23] As we saw in chapter 8, the cardinal virtues do not by themselves direct us to our final end, since they are concerned with the order in ourselves and our relation to society. We cannot have perfect virtue without charity, since it directs them to our final end.[24]

Charity not only directs us to our proper end but is also the root of the virtues. Quoting St. Gregory the Great (Homilies on the Gospel 27), he says that all the virtues come forth from charity as the branches of a tree do from one root: "as many branches come forth from one root, so many virtues are generated from one root."[25] And the root of charity, as we have seen above, is grace. Although there is a tendency today to confuse grace with charity and simply call grace "love," grace is not the same as charity. For one thing, grace *precedes* charity, as we cannot have charity unless it is poured into us. Second, charity is one of the virtues, which grace is not.[26] Grace differs from the virtues, because a virtue may only be a natural disposition for acting well but grace raises it to a higher level, above nature. It is not our own efforts but grace that makes us pleasing to God. We need grace to heal human nature that has been wounded by sin, because our natural virtues cannot do this by themselves, for they only come from the nature that needs healing.[27]

Since we only have charity because it is poured into us, it does not depend on us but on God. Thus, it is possible to lose all charity by one act that is totally contrary to the love of God. Here Christian ethics differs from any purely rational or natural ethics, for Aristotle did not think that a single act could altogether destroy a virtue, which was for him by definition a settled disposition. Someone might commit an act of injustice without ceasing to be a just person, in Aristotle's view. But for the Christian, one may lose all grace, and so all the virtues infused with it, by a single act that excludes the love of God. St. Thomas compares this with the light of the sun: God infuses virtue as the sun pours its light into the air; as it is dark when the sun is excluded from view, so grace can be lost altogether when something quite contrary to charity is done.[28]

St. Thomas differed from the Master of the *Sentences*, Peter Lombard, who held that charity is simply uncreated grace as it is the indwelling of the Holy Spirit. St. Thomas, however, thought that charity must also be something created in us or else there would be no room left for a free movement of the will. Unless there is also a movement of the will on our part in loving God, charity would be a less perfect act than our other acts of virtue. But this cannot be so, because charity especially inclines us to the good.[29] Charity must anyway also come from a movement of our will, because it is of its very nature voluntary; charity cannot be compelled. The presence of the Holy Spirit in a person does not take away the free movement of the will but makes it more free. In St. Thomas's view, our virtuous acts are wholly God's and wholly ours, not partly ours and partly God's. Thus, he differed from Pelagius before him, and Luther after him, holding to a middle way between them. Pelagius thought that they are wholly ours; Luther that they are wholly God's and we merely passive when moved by grace, since the will has been left powerless by sin. St. Thomas, on the other hand, held firmly to the initiative of God's grace in all our good actions, against Pelagius, but thought that more natural good remains in the powers of human nature since the Fall than Luther allowed.

Created charity is our participation in the divine love.[30] Thus, St. Thomas links charity closely with the Trinity. Charity is poured into us by the Holy Spirit, who has been given to us, as we noted above. The Holy Spirit is himself the Love who precedes from the Father and the Son in their loving of one another. We share in the love that the Father and the Son have for one another by charity. Thus, we are taken by charity into the very love of the divine Persons. As we noted at the end of chapter 4, our charity is a participation in the infinite Charity, who is the Holy Spirit.[31]

Love of God and Neighbor

Contrary to a widespread view at the present time, charity is not merely benevolence: what distinguishes charity from benevolence, according to St. Thomas, is that charity unites the mind with God.[32] Charity cannot merely be benevolence, because it is not just human love but is infused by God. Charity is God's love of us and our love of God. Love adds the union of affection to benevolence, St. Thomas says.[33]

As the Great Commandment of charity is twofold, to love God and our neighbor, the question arises whether charity is one virtue or two when it has two objects: God and others. St. Thomas replies that it is one virtue: its unity lies herein, that we love God for himself and everyone else as they are in God or capable of being in him. We love God in loving our neighbor when we love others as they are related to him.[34] It might appear that, if I truly love God first, I cannot love others wholeheartedly. Or we may worry that our love of others takes away from our love of God. There need be no conflict, however, between the love of God and of friends. Love of God with our whole heart does not diminish but should enhance our love of others: first, because we will also want the greatest good for our friends, which is to share in the good that God has to communicate to us, and so ultimately in beatitude; second, because the love of God enables us to be friends with others all the more, as it is the source of those feelings that are a part of friendship. As Raïssa Maritain has beautifully expressed this:

> I was to learn through experience that these particular devotions (to the saints) come into being in the same way as admiration and friendship. And in no case can friendship, which is a very gentle virtue, diminish the love with which one loves God.[35]

As friendship is of its nature a reciprocal love (there is no friendship unless each loves the other), and St. Thomas defines charity as a kind of friendship, we may wonder how acts of benevolence, which certainly show a love of neighbor, fit into his view of charity, since benevolence can be a one-sided love that is not reciprocated by the person who benefits. Although charity is more than benevolence, benevolence is part of charity because for charity it is sufficient to want the good of the other person, even though the other may not have the same love for the one wishing well. As we noted, Aristotle's third kind of friendship, the honorable, wants the good of the other person. But, as St. Thomas points out, even when the love does not appear to be reciprocal, the poor are usually grateful. In St. Thomas's view, love of the poor counts as the charity of friendship, although it may not be a reciprocal love, because it is the love of others as they are loved by God: it is to be friends with the friends of God.

Charity enables us to love others in a way that does not conflict with the love of God, because it directs our love of others toward him. As St. Thomas says, charity directs all our affections toward God. It is by the same act that we love God and others, just as we see light and colors in that light by the same act. The love of friends only conflicts with the love of God when we make them our end instead of God.[36] We love God before others, because he is the source of our happiness; and we love others as ourselves, which is to want the same good for them as we want for ourselves. We love God for the good on which the friendship of charity is founded, and others in wanting for them an association in this same good. Although charity runs through all the virtues, because it directs them to our final end and the other virtues are infused with charity, nevertheless charity is a distinct virtue, St. Thomas argues, because the virtue that orders all the others to our last end cannot itself be one of them.[37]

Wisdom and Contemplation

The end of human life, St. Thomas says, is contemplation: "Contemplation of the divine is the end of the whole of human life."[38] Does this mean that St. Thomas regards the intellect as more important than love? When we hear mention of contemplation, we think of prayer, but St. Thomas uses the word more in the sense that it had for the ancient philosophers, which was to consider any truth. It is connected with *theoria*, which comes from the Greek word for "to look at, to behold." What distinguishes the intellectual consideration of truths by the pagan philosophers from contemplation in St. Thomas is the dimension of charity. Contemplation is more simply beholding than philosophical inquiry. Also contemplation is of *divine* truth. St. Thomas agrees with St. Gregory the Great in placing contemplation on the affective rather than intellectual side, because its motive is affection. Although in itself it is an act of the intellect, we are moved to it by love, and its end lies in affection. Thus, contemplation begins and ends with love. The contemplative life consists in charity, although it considers truth with the intellect, because it results in delight and the intellect is moved by the appetite because of love.[39] Also the delight we have in the vision of the object we love stirs up in us further love. Contemplation ends in affection, because we are all delighted when we obtain what we love. We noted in chapter seven that contemplation brings us the greatest joy in this life. Although St. Thomas emphasizes the intellect, and so differs from his Franciscan contemporary at Paris, St. Bonaventure, who puts the emphasis rather on the will and love, he too thinks that love is more important in the end, for he says that the truth is to be loved more than known.[40] He says that in things beneath us knowledge is more important than love, but in things above us, where our knowledge must remain imperfect, love counts for more than knowledge.

As contemplation considers divine truth, it belongs to wisdom, for the wise man, St. Thomas says, following Aristotle, considers the highest of all causes. St. Thomas ascribes to contemplation of the truth the same qualities that scripture ascribes to wisdom: "nothing is bitter in her company; nor is there any boredom but only gladness and joy" (Wis 8:16). We find contemplation delightful, because we delight in the truth as everyone naturally desires to know. Wisdom itself is the gift of the Holy Spirit that St. Thomas especially associates with charity. Wisdom has a certain affinity (St. Thomas says "connaturality") with divine things, and so love of them: "The wisdom that has a connaturality with the divine things it judges is a gift of the Holy Spirit, because this connaturality for divine things comes from charity, which unites us with God."[41] Thus, as scripture says, wisdom makes us friends with God (Wis 7:14), because it goes with charity. By making us sharers in his wisdom, God reveals his secrets to us, St. Thomas says in his commentary on St. John. This is the true sign of friendship, that someone reveals the secret of his or her heart to a friend.[42]

Charity leads us to contemplation, because "what we seek most of all in prayer is to be united with God."[43] Charity, St. Thomas says, implies union with God.[44] It is in every way the virtue of union, for it unites us in ourselves, with others, and with God. In ourselves, as charity unites and directs all the other virtues. As we saw earlier in this chapter, to love others we have to love ourselves, for we are friends to others as we are to ourselves. To love ourselves is to love our true good, which is to have a care for virtue. The virtuous person is integrated in him or herself. The more we are friends to ourselves, the more we can be friends to others. Charity is the only one of the three supernatural virtues that unites us immediately with God. If faith did this, it would no longer be faith, which is in things not seen, but clear vision. Hope does not unite us directly with God, because we only hope for what we do not yet possess. Charity itself is perfected in the vision of God face-to-face.[45] It is not the understanding by itself but love that gives us the sight of God. Charity is perfected by a vision of the divine light, and the more we participate in charity the more we shall participate in the light of glory, so that whoever has more charity will see God more perfectly.[46] In one way our love of God can never be perfect: we can never love God perfectly, because he is infinite. But charity can be perfect, St. Thomas says, in the sense that we love God with all our strength. We are to love God without measure, for God is without limit.[47]

In this life, however, perfect charity is hindered by four things: inclinations of the mind contrary to charity; involvement in worldly affairs; attention to the needs of life, like eating

and sleeping; and heaviness of the body, which affects prompt-
ness in charity. St. Thomas thought that it is within our power to
overcome the first two obstacles, but we shall never be entirely
free from the third and fourth in this life.[48] Likewise we can only
have contemplation imperfectly in this life, because we do not
yet see clearly but only as in a mirror, with faith.[49]

Our end, St. Thomas says, is to rise by knowledge and love
above the whole order of created things and so come to the
source of all things, which is God.[50] Thus, our end brings us
back to the beginning. The end of our journey in this life is to
pass beyond the enquiry of reason to loving contemplation of
the First Truth. The way to this end is Christ, who called himself
the Way and the Truth.[51] It was for love of him that St. Thomas
said, a few days before he died, he had studied, kept watch in
prayer, toiled, taught, and preached. Now he enjoys in eternity
the blessed vision of that truth he longed to see in this life, with
the friendship of the saints.

Glossary

Accident
Accidents in Aristotle are the qualities of things, which may vary without changing the nature of a thing. It is part of human nature to have a nose, but noses can be of different shapes (straight, aquiline, etc.) without varying the species. In the Eucharist accidents are the qualities perceived by the senses: shape, texture, taste, color. Aristotle contrasts accidents with substance: a substance exists by itself; accidents exist in substances.

Actuality
Actual is contrasted with potential. Something may have a power that remains potential unless it is realized. A tulip bulb grows into an actual tulip when it is planted in some earth and receives water and light. A caterpillar is a potential butterfly.

Matter is made into something actual by receiving form. Matter never exists on its own as bare matter, so to speak, but always with the form of something or other: for example, of steel, of a sword, of iodine, or bone.

The form of a living body, according to Aristotle and Aquinas, is its soul, because the soul is the principle of life. No body is a living body without this, because not all matter is living by itself. Thus, Aristotle calls the soul the actuality of the body, because an animal or plant does not exist unless it is alive, and its principle of life, the soul, makes it alive.

Being
St. Thomas gives being (*ens*) two meanings (*ST* 1a 48:2 ad 2): (1) as it is something real, (2) as it is true of something that has being. These two can be understood by comparing sight with blindness. Blindness has being in that it is not an illusion: some things are really, or truly, blind. But it only has being in the second way, for it is not anything real in itself but only true of real things, like human beings. Blindness in itself is rather the deficiency or absence of something real, for it takes away from its full being. Sight, on the other hand, also has being in the first way.

205

Everything we think of at least has being in the mind, but not every being has actual existence. A mythical beast, like a unicorn, is a being of the mind but does not have actual existence.

Essence
Essence is equivalent to the nature of a thing. Everything has a nature, including God. The form gives a thing its essence. For example, the form of a human being is the soul, but the soul is not the essence of a human being, because it is part of the nature of a human being also to be a body. We do not speak of God having a form, only a nature or essence. Essence says what a thing is; existence that it is.

Existence
St. Thomas defines existence as "the actuality of every form or nature" (ST 1a 3:4, 4:1 ad 3). For example, the form of a horse makes something be, or exist as, an actual horse. Things may exist in the mind or in reality; only the latter have actual existence.

We contrast existence with essence, because we can know what something is without knowing whether any such thing exists in reality. Someone may know, for example, what a dodo is without knowing that dodos no longer exist.

Form
All created things have a form, if they are material, or, if they are immaterial beings like angels, they are forms. Gold has one form; copper another. These are substantial forms. Natural things have substantial forms. A different form makes copper into a kettle or a pipe. These are accidental forms, because copper can have this or that accidental form without its nature as copper being changed. Artificial things have accidental forms. Wood does not cease to be wood, its substantial form, whether it is a door or a boat, accidental forms. The form of a thing makes matter be the kind of thing that it is.

Plato thought that the forms of things existed on their own as immaterial objects in another, invisible world, only perceived by the intellect, and that things in this world are what they are by sharing in these forms. Thus, all horses share in the horse form, and lions in the lion form. Many lions share in a common form. Likewise, what makes things beautiful, according to Plato, is that they share in beauty. As Plato thought that we do not just know beautiful things but can know what beauty itself is, which is to have the idea of beauty, the Forms are also the Ideas of Plato. Thus, the Forms, or Ideas, are like the essences of things, what things are in themselves, in Plato's theory. These are immaterial, because material things are changing but the idea of, say, a horse does not change.

Aristotle, however, pointed out that the forms cannot be the essences of things when part of the essence of material things is to be bodies. What a horse is cannot be an immaterial Form or Idea when it is the nature of a horse to have a body. So Aristotle said that the forms of material things do not exist on their own separately from the things of which they are the forms, as Plato thought, but only have real existence in individual things in this world, which Aristotle said are the real things rather than the Ideas in another world. Forms also exist in the mind—for example, of a horse when I think of a horse—but this is not its real or actual existence.

Hypostasis

Hypostasis in Aquinas means the same as "person" when he is talking of the Trinity or Christ. A person, for Aquinas, is an individual subject (*suppositum*) of intelligent nature.

Idea

Since Descartes, idea has come to mean many things, for which St. Thomas uses quite distinct terms. Ideas for Locke include sense impressions, mental images, and concepts. St. Thomas uses *phantasma* (an appearance) for sense impressions, *species* for mental likenesses, and *ratio* for the concept of something. He keeps "idea" for the divine ideas. God has an idea of everything he makes, just as an artist first has an idea in his mind of what he intends to produce. In this Aquinas's use of idea is close to that of Plato, whose Ideas are like the exemplars of things. The difference is that Plato thought the Ideas exist independently on their own, but Aquinas, in the mind of God.

Neoplatonism

Neoplatonism is described in chapter two. Some of the chief Neoplatonists were Plotinus (AD 205–270), Porphyry, and Prochus (AD 410–485). Neoplatonism is a philosophic system, which describes how the world was produced through a series of beings or intelligences emanating from the One.

Participation

Plato thought that all visible things are what they are by sharing in the Forms, which are therefore the causes of things existing as what they are. A tortoise is a tortoise because it shares in the Form of a tortoise. The Tortoise Form, in Plato's theory, is the source, and so cause, of things being tortoises.

As Aquinas says, everything that has a beginning of existence, that is, all created things, receives its existence from something that already has existence. Thus, it shares, or participates in existence, for nothing can receive what does not already exist before it. Aquinas said that everything that receives its existence from another must go back to something that does not receive its existence and, therefore, simply its Existence. If God shared in existence, he would receive it. But, as he is the First Cause, not preceded by any other cause, he is Existence itself. God is Being itself, and everything else is a being by participation (*ST* 1a 3:4).

For Aquinas, we also share in the divine nature and life by grace.

Subsistent

Something is subsistent when it subsists. It subsists when it can exist in its own right, so to speak: that is, independently, by itself. A subsistent thing exists *per se* rather than through another. A table subsists, but its surface does not, because surfaces do not exist on their own but as the surface of something, a table or a wall. Thoughts do not subsist, because thoughts do not exist on their own but only in minds. God's thought, however, is subsistent, because it is identical with his mind.

Individual material things, like plants, pebbles, and boxes, are subsistent. Angels are subsistent, because they are individual beings with a mind and will of their own. Aquinas also thought that human souls are subsistent, although they are the form of the body, because they can exist on their own when separated from the body at death. This is because they have an activity of their own which is not the power of a bodily organ: this is thinking. The soul does not exist through the body but the body through the soul, which is its principle of life, and so gives the body its existence.

If pinkness existed on its own it would be subsistent; but it does not, because nothing is just pink without also being something else, for example, a flamingo or a camellia. But God is subsistent Being, because he is Being or Existence itself.

Notes

Prologue
1. I follow J. P. Torrell, OP, the latest authority for the dating of the life and works of St. Thomas.
2. Acts 17:34.
3. *CG III* 131–134.
4. See J. P. Torrell, OP, *St. Thomas Aquinas* (Washington, DC: Catholic University of America Press, 1996), vol. 1, 197.

Chapter One, How Can We Know God?
1. *ST* 1a q.3 prologue.
2. Ibid. 1a 12:13 ad 1.
3. *De Div. Nom.* c.1 lect.1, paragraph 36 in Marietti edition.
4. Ibid. c.1 lect.1 (7–9).
5. *CG* I c.3.
6. *An Essay Concerning Human Understanding* (1690) II c.4: 5.
7. *De Div. Nom.*, Aquinas, c.1 lect.1 (11).
8. Ibid. c.1 lect.2 (45).
9. *The Guide of the Perplexed* I c.54.
10. Ibid. I 58.
11. *De Pot.* 7:5.
12. *ST* 1a 13:3.
13. *De Div. Nom.* c.1 lect.2 (53).
14. *ST* 1a 13:1.
15. *De Div. Nom.* c.1 lect.2 (53).
16. Ibid. c.1 lect.2 (54).
17. *ST* 1a 13:4.
18. Ibid 1a 3:4.
19. Ex 3:14.
20. *ST* 1a 13:11.
21. Ibid 1a 13:5.
22. *De Div. Nom.* c.1 lect. 1 (30).
23. *CG* I c14.
24. *A Grammar of Assent* (1870; Longman, Green, 1947), 100.
25. 2 Cor 12:4.

26. *De Div. Nom.* c.1 lect.2 (64).
27. *Super Librum Boetii de Trinitate Proem.* q.1:2 ad 1. St. Thomas wrote his commentary on the *De Trinitate of Boethius* in Paris, 1257–58.
28. *ST* 1a 12:1 ad 3.
29. *Super Librum Boetii de Trin.* lect.1 q.1:1 ad 4.
30. *De Div. Nom.* c.1 lect.1 (8). Cf. 1 Cor 13:12.
31. *Super Librum Boetii de Trin.* Proem. q.1:2.
32. Ibid. q.6:1.
33. Ibid. Proem. q.2:1 ad 6.
34. *De Div. Nom.* c.1 lect.2 (44).
35. Is 45:15.

Chapter Two, Creation
1. *ST* 1a 3:4.
2. *De Pot* 3:5.
3. Ibid. 3:1.
4. *ST* 1a 45:5.
5. *De Pot.* 3:16.
6. *ST* 1a 65:3.
7. *De Substantiis Separatis* c.10:57.
8. *De Pot.* 3:1 ad 17.
9. *ST* 1a 45:4 ad 1.
10. *CG* III c.69.
11. *ST* 1a 45:4.
12. Ibid. 1a 65:3.
13. *De Substantiis Separatis* 59.
14. *De Pot* 3:4 ad 2.
15. *De Pot.* 3:4.
16. *CG* II c.23
17. Ibid. II c.24.
18. *De Pot.* 3:16.
19. *Ethics* prop. 33.
20. *ST* 1a 25:3 ad 2.
21. Ibid. 15:2.
22. Ibid. 1a 8:1.
23. *De Pot.* 3:6.

24. *Super Job* c.XI, ed. Leonine 76.
25. *After Aquinas* (Blackwell 2002) 40. Cf. F. Kerr.
26. *Aquinas on Doctrine* (ed. T. Weinandy) 60. Cf. ST 1a 45: 6.
27. *Physics* VIII c.1; *Metaphysics* XII c.6.
28. *ST* 1a 46:1 and 2.

Chapter Three, Good and Evil

1. *Republic* 509.
2. *ST* 1a 5:1.
3. Ibid. 1a 5:2.
4. *Pseudo-Dionysius and the Metaphysics of Aquinas* (Brill 1992), 113.
5. 1 Tm 4:4.
6. *ST* 1a 6:3.
7. *De Div Nom* c. 4 lect.16.
8. *ST* 1a 5:1.
9. *De Ver.* 21:2.
10. *Nicomachean Ethics* I c.1, 1094 a2.
11. *ST* 1a 6:3.
12. Ibid. 1a 44:4 ad 3.
13. Ibid. 1a 6:1 ad 2.
14. *De Div. Nom.* 4:14.
15. *De Pot.* 3:1.
16. *De Malo* 1:3.
17. *De Div. Nom.* 4:19.
18. Ibid. 4:22.
19. Ibid. 4:22.
20. *ST* 1a 11:2.
21. *De Div. Nom.* 4:14.
22. *ST* 1a 2ae 39:4.
23. Ibid. 1a 2ae 39:4 ad 1, ad 3.
24. *De Malo* 1:5.
25. Ibid. 2:11.
26. *Super Job* c.13 lect.1. St. Thomas wrote his commentary on Job in Orvieto, 1261–64.
27. *De Div. Nom.* 4:23.
28. *De Div. Nom.* 4:22.
29. Ibid. c.4 lect.1 (287).
30. Ibid. c.4 lect.5 (353).
31. *ST* 1a 5:4 ad1.
32. *De Div. Nom.* c.4 lect.5 (354).
33. *ST* 1a 2ae 112:1.
34. Anna Williams has written on the theme of our deification by grace in *The Ground of Union* (New York: Oxford University Press, 1999). She notes that beatitude in Aquinas includes deiformity, being made like God (p. 46).

Chapter Four, Word and Image

1. *De Trinitate* XIV c.8:11.
2. *De Pot.* 9:5.
3. *De Trinitate* IX c.12
4. *De Ver.* 10:1.
5. *De Pot.* 9:5.
6. *Super Ioannem* c.1 lect.1.
7. Ibid.
8. *De Ver.* 4:1 ad 1.
9. *De Pot.* 9:5.
10. *De Ver.* 4:2 ad 3.
11. Ibid. 4:4.
12. *ST* 1a 34:2 ad 4.
13. *De Pot.* 9:3 ad 1.
14. *Super Ioannem* c.1 lect.1.
15. Ibid. c.1 lect.2.
16. *De Ver.* 4:4.
17. *ST* la 43:5 ad 2.
18. *De Trinitate* IX 10 L "verbum est . . . cum amore notitia."
19. *CG* IV c.19:10.
20. *ST* 1a 37:2 ad 3.
21. *CG* IV c.19.
22. *De Pot.* 9:9.
23. *CG* IV c.11.
24. *ST* 1a 42:5.
25. *Super Ioannem* c.XIV lect.6 (1946).
26. Anna Williams remarks that all sanctification comes under "the mission of the Trinity" (*The Ground of Union*, 64). Although grace comes to us through the humanity of Christ united to his divine nature, the Incarnation

takes us back to the Trinity as the visible mission of the Son. What we call "sanctifying grace" is called by St. Thomas "grace that makes one pleasing" to God.
27. *ST* 1a 43:5 ad 2.
28. Ibid. 1a 43:5 ad 3.
29. Cf. Phil 3:10.
30. *CG* IV c.22.
31. *Super Ioannem* XIV lect.6 (1958).
32. *De Ver.* 10:7 ad 7.
33. *ST* 2a 2ae 24:5 ad 3.

Chapter Five, Angels

1. *De Substantiis Separatis* c.14:79. This treatise was written in Paris in the second half of 1271, so a few years after the first part of the *Summa Theologiae*.
2. *ST* 1a 50:1.
3. Cf. Acts 23:8.
4. *De Malo* 16:1.
5. *De Substantiis Separatis* 8:45.
6. *De Pot.* 3:13; *ST* 1a 61:3.
7. *Leviathan* I c.4.
8. *Metaphysics* VII c.8 1033 b 16.
9. *De Ver.* 10:1 ad 4.
10. *De Trinitate* IX c.8.
11. Heb 13:2; cf. Gn 18:2.
12. *ST* 1a 51:2 ad 1.
13. *De Ver.* 8:9.
14. *ST* 1a 56:1.
15. *Ad Eph.* c.1 lect.7 (62).
16. *ST* 1a 108:6.
17. Ibid. 1a 113:2.
18. Ibid. 1a 50:4.
19. Ibid. 57:1.
20. *De Ver.* 9:1.
21. Ibid. 9:4.
22. Ibid. 9:5.
23. *ST* 1a 52:3.
24. Sonnet 44.
25. *ST* 1a 63:4.
26. *De Malo* 16:2.
27. *De Div. Nom.* c.4 lect.19.
28. *ST* 1a 63:3.
29. *De Malo* 16:3.
30. Ibid. 16:5.
31. *ST* 1a 62:5.
32. Ibid. 1a 64:2.
33. *De Malo* 16:5.

Chapter Six, The Soul

1. *The Metaphysics of Mind* (Oxford: Oxford University Press, 1989), 46.
2. Ibid. 17 and 32.
3. *Commentarium in De Anima* I lect.1. St. Thomas's commentary on the *De Anima* of Aristotle is to be distinguished from his own *Questions on the Soul*.
4. Aquinas' Rejection of Mind, *Thomist* 66 (2002): 15–59.
5. *De Ver.* 10:1 ad 4.
6. *ST* 1a 75:1.
7. *De Pot.* 3:10 ad 16.
8. *ST* 1a 76:1.
9. *Quodlibet* 2:1,1.
10. *ST* 1a 75:2.
11. *De Ver.* 10:8.
12. *ST* 1a 75:5 ad 1.
13. *The Foundations of Arithmetic*, 34.
14. *De Anima* III c.5, 430a 25.
15. *De Unitate Intellectus* 14.
16. *Comm. In De Anima* III lect.7.
17. *ST* 1a 84:7.
18. *De Pot.* 3:9 ad 22.
19. *ST* 1a 75:3.
20. *De Ente et Essentia* c.5.
21. *ST* 1a 75:6.
22. *Quaestiones de Anima* 1 ad 14. St. Thomas wrote his *Questions on the Soul* in Rome, 1265–66.
23. *Immortality and Pre-existence* (London 1915) 58f.
24. *ST* 1a 75:6.
25. *ST* 1a 90:2 ad 2.
26. Cf. *De Generatione Animalium* II c.3, 736b 28.
27. *ST* 1a 118:2.

28. *Super Ioannem* c.1 lect.5 (129).
29. *De Ver.* 10:1.
30. *ST* 1a 79:4.
31. Ibid. 1a 77:1.
32. Ibid. 1a 77:5 ad 1.
33. *Quaestiones. de Anima* 12.
34. *Thomistic Papers* (Houston 1984), vol. 1, 90.
35. *Quaestiones de Anima* 1 ad 12.
36. Ibid. q.10.
37. *ST* 1a 76:1.
38. *CG* II c.50.
39. *Quaestiones de Anima* q.1 (central reply, last paragraph).
40. Ibid. q.1 ad 2.
41. *God and the Soul* (London: Routledge & Kegan Paul, 1969), 28.
42. *ST* 1a 76:1 ad 6.
43. Ibid. 1a 29:1 ad 5.
44. Ibid. 1a 75:4.

Chapter Seven, The Emotions

1. *ST* 1a 2ae 37:4 ad 1.
2. Ibid. 1a 2ae 48:4.
3. Ibid. 1a 2ae 22:3. Cf. *De Fide Orthodoxa* II c.22.
4. *ST* 1a 2ae 24:2.
5. Ibid. 1a 2ae 59:2 ad 5.
6. Ibid. 1a 2ae 24:1.
7. *Qq. de Virt.* 4.
8. *ST* 1a 2ae 34:1; 34:3.
9. Ibid. 1a 2ae 24:3.
10. Ibid. 1a 2ae 23:3 ad 1.
11. Ibid. 1a 2ae 23:2.
12. Ibid. 1a 2ae 40:4 ad 3.
13. Ibid. 1a 2ae 23:2.
14. *De Ver.* 26:4.
15. *ST* 1a 2ae 26:1; 25:2.
16. Ibid. 1a 2ae 36:1.
17. Ibid. 1a 2ae 29:5.
18. Ibid. 1a 2ae 29:3 ad 1.
19. Ibid. 1a 2ae 29:1.
20. Ibid. 1a 2ae 41:2 ad 1.
21. Ibid. 1a 2ae 26:1; 27:1.
22. Ibid. 1a 2ae 28:5.
23. Ibid. 1a 2ae 28:1 ad 2.
24. Ibid. 1a 2ae 28:2.
25. Ibid. 1a 2ae 35:2.
26. Ibid. 1a 2ae 31:3.
27. *Ethics* X c.7.
28. *ST* 1a 2ae 38:4.
29. Ibid. 1a 2ae 32:8 ad 2.
30. *Ethics* VII c.14, 1154b28.
31. *ST* 1a 2ae 32:6.
32. Ibid. 1a 2ae 32:7 ad 2.
33. Ibid. 1a 2ae 35:5.
34. Ibid. 1a 2ae 32:7 ad 3.
35. Ibid. 1a 2ae 32:1 ad 3.
36. Ibid. 1a 2ae 31:6.
37. Ibid. 1a 2ae 27:1 ad 3.
38. Ibid. 1a 2ae 36:3.
39. Ibid. 1a 2ae 37:2.
40. Ibid. 1a 2ae 37:1; 33:3.
41. Ibid. 1a 2ae 37:1 ad 3.
42. Ibid. 1a 2ae 35:7 ad 2.
43. Ibid. 1a 2ae 35:8.
44. Ibid. 1a 2ae 37:2.
45. Ibid. 1a 2ae 35:4 ad 3.
46. Ibid. 1a 2ae 37:2.
47. Ibid. 1a 2ae 38:1.
48. Ibid. 1a 2ae 32:5.
49. Ibid. 1a 2ae 35:8 ad 3.
50. Ibid. 1a 2ae 32:4.
51. Ibid. 1a 2ae 39:4 ad 3.
52. Ibid. 1a 2ae 39:4 ad 1.
53. Ibid. 1a 2ae 38:2 ad 1.
54. *Ethics* IX c.11.
55. Ibid. 1a 2ae 38:3.
56. Ibid. 1a 2ae 38:4.
57. Ibid.
58. Ibid. 1a 2ae 38:2.
59. ibid 1a 2ae 38:1.
60. Ibid. 1a 2ae 38:5 ad 3.
61. Ibid. 1a 2ae 46:5.
62. Ibid. 1a 2ae 29:6.
63. Ibid. 1a 2ae 47:1 ad 2.
64. Ibid. 1a 2ae 44:4.
65. Ibid. 1a 2ae 46:5.
66. Ibid. 2a 2ae 157:4.

67. Ibid. 1a 2ae 47:4.
68. Ibid. 1a 2ae 48:3 ad 3.
69. Ibid. 1a 2ae 47:1 ad 3.
70. Ibid. 1a 2ae 47:1 ad 2.
71. Ibid. 1a 2ae 46:2.
72. Ibid. 1a 2ae 46:1 ad 3.
73. Ibid. 1a 2ae 48:1.
74. *De Ver.* 26:4.
75. *Qq. de Virt.*; cf. Aristotle, *Politics* I c.3.
76. *ST* 1a 2ae 59:1.

Chapter Eight, The Virtues

1. *ST* 1a 2ae 58:1.
2. *Qq. de Virt.* 13.
3. Ibid. 12.
4. *ST* 1a 2ae 58:3 ad 3.
5. Ibid. 1a 2ae 62:1 ad 1.
6. *Qq. de Virt.* 12 ad 24.
7. Ibid. 1.
8. *After Aquinas* 133.
9. *ST* 1a 2ae 1:5.
10. *Disputed Questions on Virtue*, trans. Ralph McInerny (Bloomington: Indiana University Press, 1999), xviii. Cf. *ST* 11 1a 2ae 5:5; 3:2 ad 4.
11. *ST* 1a 2ae 16:1.
12. *ST* 1a 2ae 13:2.
13. Ibid. 1a 2ae 6:3.
14. Ibid. 1a 2ae 6:4 ad 1.
15. Ibid. 1a 2ae 9:6 ad 3.
16. Ibid. 1a 2ae 9:4 ad 2
17. Ibid. 1a 2ae 6:7 ad 1.
18. Ibid. 1a 2ae 6:8.
19. Ibid. 1a 2ae 8:3 ad 3.
20. Ibid. 1a 2ae 13:5 ad 1.
21. Ibid. 1a 2ae 9:2 ad 2.
22. Ibid. 1a 2ae 6:4 ad 2.
23. Ibid. 1a 2ae 10:2.
24. Ibid. 1a 2ae 13:6.
25. Ibid. 1a 2ae 9:5 ad 3.
26. Ibid. 1a 2ae 57:5; 2a 2ae 47:2.
27. Ibid. 2a 2ae 49:8.
28. Ibid. 2a 2ae 47:8.
29. Ibid. 2a 2ae 51:1 ad 3.
30. Ibid. 2a 2ae 47:13; *Question About the Cardinal Virtues* 2 ad 3.
31. *ST* 2a 2ae 55:7 ad 2.
32. Ibid. 2a 2ae 55:6.
33. Ibid. 1a 2ae 12:4 ad 3.
34. Ibid. 1a 2ae 19:8.
35. *The Merchant of Venice* act 1 sc.2 line 16.
36. *ST* 2a 2ae 49:3.
37. *Qq. de Virt.* 6 ad 1.
38. *ST* 1a 2ae 66:5 ad 1.
39. Ibid. 1a 2ae 65:2.
40. *Qq. De Virtutibus Cardinalibus* 2; cf. *Moralia in Job* XXII c.1.
41. *ST* 1a 2ae 65:1 ad 3.
42. *Qq. de Virt.* 12 ad 17.
43. Aristotle, *Ethics* III c.5, 1114a 31.
44. *ST* 1a 2ae 61:4.
45. Ibid. 1a 2ae 65:1.
46. *Qq. de Virt.* 9 ad 16.
47. *The Recovery of Virtue* (Louisville 1990) 169.
48 *Qq. de Virt.* 6.
49. *ST* 2a 2ae 58:12.
50. Ibid. 2a 2ae 58:2.
51. Ibid. 2a 2ae 61:1.
52. Ibid. 2a 2ae 77:1-4.
53. Ibid. 2a 2ae 67:2.
54. Ibid. 2a 2ae 109:3.
55. Ibid. 2a 2ae 109:1 ad 3.
56. Ibid. 2a 2ae 109:4.
57. *Qq. de Virt.* 5.
58. Porter, *The Recovery of Virtue*, 127.
59. *ST* 2a 2ae 123:2.
60. Ibid. 1a 2ae 61:3.
61. *Qq. De Virtutibus Cardinalibus* 4 ad 2.
62. *Qq. de Virt.* 9.
63. Ibid. 10 ad 8.
64. *ST* 1a 2ae 63:4.
65. Ibid. 1a 2ae 65:3.
66. *Super I ad Tim.* c.1 lect.2 (16).
67. *ST* 1a 2ae 65:3.
68. *Qq. de Virtutibus Cardinalibus* 4.
69. *ST* 1a 2ae 67:1.

Chapter Nine, The Old Law

1. *ST* 2a 2ae 10:12.
2. Ibid. 2a 2ae 10:11.
3. *Ad Galatos* c.3 lect.7 (167).
4. *ST* 1a 2ae 98:4.
5. Ibid. 1a 2ae 100:1.
6. Ibid. 1a 2ae 91:1.
7. Ibid. 1a 2ae 91:2.
8. Ibid. 1a 2ae 93:2.
9. *After Aquinas* 104.
10. *ST* 1a 2ae 94:2.
11. Ibid 1a 2ae 94:4. Cf. *De Bello Gallico* VI 23.
12. Law, Virtue and Happiness in Aquinas' Moral Theory, *Thomist* 61 (1997): 429.
13. Ibid. 442.
14. *ST* 1a 2ae 99:1 ad 1.
15. Ibid. 1a 2ae 98:2 ad 3.
16. *Ad Galatos* c.3 lect.7 (165).
17. *ST* 1a 2ae 99:2.
18. Ibid. 1a 2ae 99:1 ad 2.
19. Ibid. 1a 2ae 100:3 ad 1.
20. Ibid. 1a 2ae 101:2; 103:3.
21. Ibid. 1a 2ae 107:1 ad 2. Cf. Rom 5:5.
22. Cf. Heb 8:5; 10:1.
23. *ST* 1a 2ae 101:3 ad 1; 102:6.
24. Ibid. 1a 2ae 101:4 ad 2.
25. Ibid. 1a 2ae 101:4 ad 2.
26. *Ad Romanos* c.6 lect. 2 (551).
27. Ibid. c.9 lect.1 (744).
28. *Ad Hebraeos* c.7 lect.3 (362).
29. Ibid. c.9 lect.3 (444).
30. *ST* 1a 2ae 107,3.
31. *Ad Galatos* c.3 lect.8.
32. *Ad Hebraeos* c.10 lect.1.
33. *Ad Romanos* c.8 lect.1 (611) on Rom 8:3.
34. *ST* 1a 2ae 106:1 ad 3.
35. Ibid. 1a 2ae 106:1 ad 2.
36. *Ad Romanos* c.7 lect.3 (557).
37. *ST* 1a 2ae 107:2. Cf. Mt 5:34.
38. Ibid. 1a 2ae 106:1.
39. *Ad Hebraeos* c.9 lect.1.

Chapter Ten, The Sacrament of Salvation

1. *Quodlibet* 2,4,6 ad 4.
2. *After Aquinas* 102.
3. *CG* IV c.32.
4. Ibid. IV c.32, 5.
5. Denzinger-Schönmetzer, *Enchiridion Symbolorum*, 301.
6. *CG* IV c.38:7. Cf. *De Fide Orthodoxa* III c.4.
7. *CG* IV c.34:22.
8 Ibid. IV c.39:13
9. *ST* 3a 2:3.
10. Ibid. 3a 2:2 and 3.
11. *Aquinas on Doctrine* 80.
12. *Quaestio de Unione Verbi Incarnati* art. 4.
13. *Ad Galatos* c.2 lect.6 (112).
14. *ST* 3a 62:6.
15. *Ad Romanos* c.4 lect.3 (380).
16. *ST* 3a 62:5 ad 3.
17. Cf. 2 Cor 5:17.
18. *Ad Hebraeos* c.10 lect.1 (488).
19. Ibid. c.10 lect.1.
20. Ibid. c.10 lect.1 (492).
21. Ibid. c.9 lect.5 (477).
22. *ST* 3a 47:2 ad 3.
23. *Ad Galatos* c.2 lect.6 (110).
24. *ST* 3a 48,1 ad 1.
25. Ibid. 3a 46:3.
26. Ibid. 3a 50:1.
27. *Ad Hebraeos* c.9 lect.5 (470).
28. *St. Thomas Aquinas* 132.
29. *ST* 3a 7,9.
30. Ibid. 3a 8,5 ad 1.
31. *Super Ioannem* c.1 lect.8 (190).
32. *ST* 3a 49:1.
33. *Super Ioannem* c.1 lect.8 (188).
34. Ibid. c.6 lect.5 (935–36).
35. Ibid. c.14 lect.2 (1874).
36. Cf. *De Fide Orthodoxa* III c.15.
37. *Ad Romanos* c.4 lect.3 (380).
38. *ST* 3a 60:6.
39. Ibid. 3a 62:5.
40. Mk 8:23.

41. *ST* 3a 62:6.
42. Ibid. 3a 48:6 ad 2.
43. Lk 8:43.
44. *De Ver.* 27:4.
45. *Ad Hebraeos* c.10 lect.1 (482).
46. *ST* 3a 73:5 ad 2.
47. Ibid. 3a 48:1.
48. Ibid. 3a 48:6 ad 3.
49. *Ad Hebraeos* c.10 lect.1 (480).
50. Ibid. c.9 lect.5 (477).
51. *ST* 3a 69,2.
52. *Quodlibet* II 2,1,2, debated in Paris, Christmas 1269.
53. *Compendium Theologiae* c.227, written in Rome, 1265–68, for his secretary, Reginald of Piperno.
54. *ST* 3a 49:1 ad 4.
55. *Ad Ephesos* c.5 lect.10 (334).
56. *ST* 3a 64:2 ad 3.
57. Ibid. 3a 64:1 ad 2.
58. Ibid. 3a 49:3 ad 3.

Chapter Eleven, The Eucharist

1. Jn 1:14.
2. *ST* 73:4 ad 3.
3. Ibid. 3a 83,1.
4. *Super 1 Corinthos* c.11 lect.5 (665).
5. *ST* 3a 75:1.
6. Ibid. 3a 77:7 ad 3.
7. Ibid. 3a 75:2.
8. Ibid. 3a 76:6.
9. Ibid. 3a 76:1 ad 3.
10. Ibid. 3a 76:6.
11. Ibid. 3a 78:5.
12. *Super I Corinthos* c.11 lect.5 (669).
13. *ST* 3a 77:1 ad 3.
14. *Pange lingua gloriosi* (Office of Corpus Christi).
15. *ST* 3a 75:4.
16. *De Sacramentis* 4:15 (ST 3a 78,4 sec contra).
17. *ST* 3a 75:4.
18. Ibid. 3a 78:5.
19. Ibid. 3a 78:2 ad 2.

20. Ibid. 3a 75:8 ad 1.
21. Ibid. 3a 75:3.
22. Ibid. 3a 76:1 ad 3.
23. Ibid. 3a 76:5.
24. Ibid. 3a 76:3.
25. *New Approaches to the Eucharist* (Dublin, 1967), 86.
26. *ST* 3a 78:5 ad 2.
27. Ibid. 3a 76:1 ad 1.
28. Ibid. 3a 76:1.
29. Ibid. 3a 76:1 ad 1.
30. *Super Ioannem* c.6 lect.6.
31. Jn 6:57.
32. *Super 1 ad Corinthos* c.11 lect. 5.
33. *Super Ioannem* c.6 lect.7.
34. *Super Habraeos* c.10 lect.2; Heb 10:20.
35. *Adoro te devote*, last verse.
36. Cf. *Lauda, Sion* (Sequence for Corpus Christi).

Chapter Twelve, The Resurrection

1. *ST* 3a 56:1 ad 2. Cf Jn 5:27.
2. *ST* 3a 56:1.
3. *Super 1 Corinthos* c.15 lect.2 (914).
4. Ibid. c.15 lect.2 (913).
5. *ST* 3a 56:1 ad 3.
6. *Compendium Theologiae* c.239.
7. *ST* 3a 55:5.
8. Ibid. 3a 54:2 ad 1.
9. Ibid. 3a 55:6.
10. *Quodlibet* 4,5,8.
11. *Super 2 Tim* 2 lect. 3 (68).
12. *Super Ioannem* c.5 lect. 5 (790).
13. *CG* IV c.79.
14. *Super I Cor* XV lect2.
15. *Super Job* XIV ed. Leonina vol.26 p.93.
16. *Super 1 Cor* XV lect.2 (924).
17. *ST* 3a 54:3 ad 1.
18. *Super 1 Cor* XV lect. 6 (984).
19. *CG* IV c.86.5.
20. *CG* IV c.84.7.

21. *Super 1 Cor* XV lect. 6 (980). Cf 1 Cor 15:37.
22. *Super 1 Cor* XV lect. 5 (970).
23. Ibid. XV lect. 6 (983).
24. *CG* IV c.86.4.
25. Ibid. IV c.84.2.
26. *ST* 3a 54:2 ad 2.
27. *De Div. Nom.* 1 lect.2 (66).
28. *Super 1 Cor* XV lect. 6 (988).
29. *CG* IV c.86 ult.
30. *Super Job* c.19, ed. Leonina vol. 26, pp116–117.
31. Ibid. XV lect.7 (991).
32. Ibid. XV lect.7 (998).
33. Ibid. XV lect. 9 (1015).
34. *CG* IV c.81,5.

Chapter Thirteen, Charity and Friendship

1. *ST* 1a 2ae 26:3 ad 4.
2. Ibid. 1a 2ae 26:4.
3. J. McEvoy and M. Dunn, eds., *Thomas Aquinas: Approaches to Truth* (Dublin: Four Courts, 2002), 20.
4. Ibid. 32. Cf Jn 15:15.
5. *In Ethicorum* VIII lect.3 (1574).
6. Ibid. VIII lect.5 (1601).
7. Ibid. VIII lect.6 (1614).
8. *Ethics* IX c.11, 1171 a 30.
9. Ibid. VIII c.5, 1157 b 20.
10. *In Ethicorum* IX lect.13 (1925).
11. Mt 22:39; Lv 19:18.
12. *Ethics* IX c.4, 1166 a 1.
13. Ibid. IX c.8, 1169 a 3.
14. Ibid. IX c.8, 1168 b 29.
15. *ST* 2a 2ae 25:7.
16. *Ethics* IX c.4, 1166a 13–20.
17. *In Symbolum Apostolorum* art. 12.
18. *Ethics* VIII c.7, 1159 a 4.
19. *ST* 2a 2ae 25:2 ad 2.
20. *Super Romanos* c.5 lect.1 (392).
21. *Super Ioannem* c.15 lect.3 (2011).
22. *De Spiritu et Littera* 32,57.
23. *ST* 2a 2ae 24:12.
24. Ibid. 2a 2ae 23:7 ad 1.

25. *Super Ioannem* c.15 lect.2 (2006).
26. See *De Ver.* 27:2: Is grace the same as charity?
27. *ST* 1a 2ae 109:9.
28. Ibid. 2a 2ae 24:12.
29. *Questiones de Caritate* 1: Is charity something created in the soul or the Holy Spirit himself?
30. *ST* 2a 2ae 24:2: Is charity infused?
31. Ibid. 2a 2ae 24:7.
32. Ibid. 2a 2ae 24:4.
33. Ibid. 2a 2ae 27:2: Is the act of charity the same as benevolence?
34. *Questiones de Caritate* 4.
35. *We Have Been Friends Together. Adventures in Grace* (Garden City, NY: Image Books, 1961), 184.
36. *ST* 2a 2ae 25:1.
37. *Questiones de Caritate* 5.
38. *ST* 2a 2ae 180:4.
39. Ibid. 2a 2ae 180:1.
40. Ibid. 2a 2ae 180:7 ad 1.
41. *ST* 2a 2ae 45:2.
42. *Super Ioannem* c.15 lect.3.
43. *ST* 2a 2ae 83:1 ad 2.
44. Ibid. 2a 2ae 24:12 ad 5.
45. *Questiones de Caritate* 10.
46. *ST* 1a 12:6.
47. *Questiones de Caritate* 2 ad 13.
48. Ibid. q.10.
49. Cf. 1 Cor 13:12.
50. *CG* II c.87.
51. Jn 14:6.

Index

Rev. Francis Selman has worked in parishes in Cambridge and Norwich, and was assistant chaplain at Cambridge University Catholic Chapláincy from 1980 to 1983. He currently teaches philosophy and theology at Allen Hall, London and Maryvale Institute, Birmingham. He is the author of *St. Thomas Aquinas, From Physics to Metaphysics*, and *The Soul—An Inquiry*.

⚬Christian⚬Classics

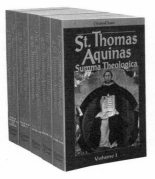

SUMMA THEOLOGICA
Complete English Edition in Five Volumes
St. Thomas Aquinas

Creating a summary of all human knowledge may not be the sort of undertaking we begin in the twenty-first century, but there is still room on our bookshelves for a classic—*Summa Theologica*, one of the world's oldest and greatest masterpieces. St. Thomas Aquinas has much to teach us—most especially how to confront the classic questions that are still with us after centuries of thought.
Complete Five-Volume Set
PAPERBACK SET ISBN: 9780870610691
3,022 pages / $165.00
HARDCOVER SET ISBN: 9780870610639
3,022 pages / $255.00

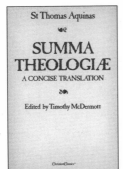

Summa Theologiae: A Concise Translation
St. Thomas Aquinas
Edited by Timothy McDermott

In his admirable new translation . . . Timothy McDermott has skillfully edited the text to about one sixth of its length.
Fergus Ker
London Tablet

The real meat of St. Thomas has been captured here with remarkable good judgement, and it is in fact a fresh stimulation experience to read Aquinas' doctrine on a given point gathered all together.
W. Norris Clarke, S.J.
Fordham University, *International Philosophical Quarterly*

PAPERBACK ISBN: 9780870612107 / 652 pages / $42.50
HARDCOVER ISBN: 9780870612114 / 652 pages / $59.95

Available from your bookstore or from
ave maria press / Notre Dame, IN 46556
www.avemariapress.com / Ph: 800-282-1865
A Ministry of the Indiana Province of Holy Cross

Keycode: FØAØ8Ø7ØØØØ